I0448585

September 2013

# GLOBAL FOOD SECURITY

# USAID Is Improving Coordination but Needs to Require Systematic Assessments of Country-Level Risks

**G A O**
Accountability * Integrity * Reliability

# Highlights

Highlights of GAO-13-809, a report to congressional requesters

## GLOBAL FOOD SECURITY
## USAID Is Improving Coordination but Needs to Require Systematic Assessments of Country-Level Risks

## Why GAO Did This Study

In fiscal years 2010 through 2013, the U.S. government allocated $7 billion to implement global food security programs implemented under the FTF initiative by USAID and its U.S. FTF partner agencies, which include the Departments of Agriculture, State, and the Treasury, and the Millennium Challenge Corporation. To enhance FTF efforts to increase agricultural productivity and reduce malnutrition in 19 chronically food insecure countries, USAID has outlined two approaches: an FTF whole-of-government approach, which aims to improve coordination and integrate expertise and resources of all FTF partner agencies, and a country-led approach to build country capacity to sustain U.S. efforts by including the host government and other stakeholders in planning and implementation.

GAO was asked to study the FTF initiative. GAO examined (1) the extent to which USAID has implemented a whole-of-government approach and (2) how USAID has facilitated a country-led approach. GAO analyzed FTF-related agency documents, conducted a survey of all USAID and U.S. FTF partner agency representatives implementing FTF in 19 focus countries, and interviewed FTF agency officials in Washington, D.C.

## What GAO Recommends

The USAID Administrator should require FTF country staff to conduct periodic risk assessments associated with pursuing a country-led approach and to develop plans to mitigate the risks identified. USAID concurred with the recommendations.

View GAO-13-809. To view an e-supplement with more data, see GAO-13-815SP. For more information, contact Thomas Melito at (202) 512-9601 or MelitoT@gao.gov.

## What GAO Found

The U.S. Agency for International Development (USAID) has made progress in coordinating with U.S. partner agencies through the whole-of-government approach for the Feed the Future (FTF) initiative that began in 2010. According to USAID documents, this approach involves coordination and integration of expertise and resources across U.S. partner agencies with global food security programs. In reports issued in 2008 and 2010, GAO found that U.S. agency food security efforts were fragmented and uncoordinated. Under FTF, GAO found that USAID leads the whole-of-government approach by better coordinating and integrating partner agencies' knowledge and expertise at three levels: at headquarters in Washington, D.C.; in each of the 19 FTF focus countries; and between the countries and headquarters. In headquarters, USAID and FTF partner agencies established joint strategies and new data management systems to track funding and results across the U.S. government. At the country level, in GAO's survey of U.S. FTF partner agency representatives in 19 FTF focus countries, 93 percent reported coordinating with USAID.

**Reported Coordination with U.S. and Country Stakeholders in the 19 FTF Countries**

Percentage of U.S. FTF partner representatives reporting coordination with USAID

| | |
|---|---|
| Percentage | 93 |

| Percentage of USAID representatives reporting coordination with | | Percentage of USAID representatives reporting working with | |
|---|---|---|---|
| Department of State | 60 | Host government | 86 |
| Department of Agriculture | 52 | Nonprofits | 79 |
| Peace Corps | 40 | Donors | 73 |
| Other | 40 | For-profits | 68 |

Note: All percentages have a margin of error of no more than plus or minus 4 percent.
Source: GAO survey.

USAID has facilitated a country-led approach but has not systematically assessed risks associated with this approach. USAID has facilitated the approach by providing assistance to the host governments in developing country plans and coordinating on FTF with country stakeholders, including nonprofit and for-profit organizations. U.S. FTF partner agency representatives answering GAO's survey reported working with multiple country stakeholders on FTF. In its March 2010 report, GAO found that the country-led approach was vulnerable to a number of risks, including insufficient capacity of host governments to meet funding commitments for agriculture. USAID has since made some progress in monitoring these risks, including tracking the number of focus countries that increase public expenditure for agriculture. However, GAO's current study found that USAID's FTF multiyear country strategies did not systematically assess risks to the country-led approach. For example, 12 of the 19 strategies did not contain sections discussing assessments of risks such as the host government's insufficient capacity and policies that inhibit private sector investment. GAO also found that fewer than half of the risks identified had corresponding discussions of mitigation strategies. Although USAID country guidance documents indicate that country teams must assess risks associated with USAID's development objectives, the agency does not require country teams to systematically assess and mitigate risks to the country-led approach. Without requirements for FTF country staff to identify and mitigate risks associated with the country-led approach, the U.S. government's ability to achieve its goals for improving global food security could be limited.

_____ **United States Government Accountability Office**

# Contents

Tables

Figures

## List of Abbreviations

| | |
|---|---|
| CAADP | Comprehensive Africa Agriculture Development Program |
| CDCS | Country Development Cooperation Strategies |
| CIP | country investment plan |
| CSO | civil society organization |
| FANEP | Food Aid Nutrition Enhancement Program |
| FTF | Feed the Future |
| FTF Guide | Feed the Future Guide |
| FTFMS | Feed the Future Monitoring System |
| FTF Scorecard | Feed the Future Scorecard |
| G8 | Group of Eight |
| G20 | Group of Twenty |
| GAFSP | Global Agriculture and Food Security Program |
| LRP | Local and Regional Procurement Pilot Project |
| MCC | Millennium Challenge Corporation |
| NGO | nongovernmental organization |
| OLS | ordinary least squares |
| OMB | Office of Management and Budget |
| OPIC | Overseas Private Investment Corporation |
| QDDR | Quadrennial Diplomacy and Development Review |
| State | Department of State |
| Treasury | Department of the Treasury |
| USADF | United States African Development Foundation |
| USAID | United States Agency for International Development |
| USDA | United States Department of Agriculture |
| USTR | Office of the United States Trade Representative |

September 17, 2013

The Honorable Eliot Engel
Ranking Member
Committee on Foreign Relations
House of Representatives

The Honorable Ileana Ros-Lehtinen
House of Representatives

The Honorable James P. McGovern
House of Representatives

Nearly 870 million people, more than one-eighth of the world's population, suffer from chronic hunger, and more than 2.5 million children die each year from undernutrition, according to the United Nations World Food Program. In 2008, the World Bank reported that numerous efforts to promote agriculture in developing countries had failed due to factors such as inefficient agriculture tax policies and underinvestment in agriculture.[1] The World Bank also reported that, in response to recurring food crises, donors had shifted their priorities toward directly providing food rather than investing in programs to increase economic growth and food security.

In 2009, recognizing that overcoming underinvestment in agriculture in the world's poorest countries would require stronger global partnerships, leaders at the Group of Eight (G8) Summit in L'Aquila, Italy, committed to increase food security assistance, and especially public and private investments in developing countries' agricultural sectors.[2] The President announced that the United States would invest at least $3.5 billion over 3

---

[1]World Bank, *World Development Report 2008: Agriculture for Development* (Washington, D.C.: 2007).

[2]The G8 is an assembly of world leaders who meet annually to discuss global issues. The leaders represent the United States, Canada, France, Germany, Italy, Japan, Russia, and the United Kingdom. The European Union is also represented by the Presidents of the European Commission and the Council. At the G8 Summit in L'Aquila, Italy, in July 2009, and the subsequent Group of Twenty (G20) Summit in Pittsburgh, Pennsylvania, in September 2009, major donor countries and the European Commission pledged to significantly increase aid to agriculture and food security.

years through the Feed the Future (FTF) initiative aimed at increasing agricultural productivity and reducing malnutrition among children in 19 chronically food insecure countries.[3]

To strengthen the effectiveness of this initiative, the President's new development policy outlined an operational model for global food security programs focused on among other things (1) enhancing the level of interagency cooperation by providing incentives for the design of common analysis, planning, and programs drawing on the perspectives and expertise of different U.S. agencies, and (2) responding to country priorities by ensuring that U.S. investments aligned with established national strategies and development plans of partner countries based on consultation with a broad range of stakeholders. In prior reports, we found that U.S. efforts to coordinate food security programs implemented by multiple federal agencies were fragmented and lacked integration and data management systems. Because of this fragmented approach to food security, the U.S. government was likely missing opportunities to leverage each agency's expertise and to minimize duplication. Furthermore, we found that coordination of agricultural development programs had been difficult at the country level due, in part, to the large number of donor agricultural development projects that were not adequately aligned. We also reported that the U.S. approach was vulnerable to a number of risks, including the weak capacity of host governments and difficulties in aligning U.S. assistance with host governments' own strategies, and recommended that State delineate measures to mitigate risks associated with the country-led approach.[4]

In fiscal years 2010 through 2013, the U.S. government, through multiple federal agencies, allocated $7 billion for global food security programs

---

[3]The U.S. global commitment was initially referred to as the Global Hunger and Food Security Initiative but came to be known as Feed the Future in May 2010 with the publication of the *Feed the Future Guide* (FTF Guide).

[4]See GAO, *International Food Security: Insufficient Efforts by Host Governments and Donors Threaten Progress to Halve Hunger in Sub-Saharan Africa by 2015*, GAO-08-680 (Washington, D.C.: May 29, 2008), and *Global Food Security: U.S. Agencies Progressing on Governmentwide Strategy, but Approach Faces Several Vulnerabilities*, GAO-10-352 (Washington, D.C.: Mar. 11, 2010). To address some of these risks, State has begun to implement this recommendation by providing support to countries in the development of their food security plans and by reviewing these plans before committing a higher level of U.S. funding.

under FTF.[5] Among other things, the initiative, led by the U.S. Agency for International Development (USAID), established a framework for a whole-of-government approach that attempts to maximize the effectiveness of interagency resources and knowledge through common goals, improved coordination, and resource alignment.[6] Additionally, FTF sought to build country capacity and sustainability by obtaining input from the host government and other stakeholders in planning and implementation efforts. This country-led approach promotes the participation of key stakeholders, with an emphasis on including not only the host government but also nonstate actors, such as advocacy groups, the private sector, and local and international nonprofit entities.[7]

You asked us to review the FTF initiative. This report addresses (1) the extent to which USAID has applied a whole-of-government approach and (2) how USAID has facilitated a country-led approach. To determine the extent to which USAID has applied FTF's whole-of-government approach and to assess how USAID has facilitated a country-led approach, we reviewed agency planning and guidance documents, surveyed USAID and U.S. FTF partner agency representatives in the 19 FTF focus countries on coordination mechanisms and stakeholder consultation, and

---

[5]Funding data are reported as of March 31, 2013.

[6]In this report, "whole-of-government" refers to FTF's approach for enhancing coordinated and comprehensive action within the U.S. government. While the May 2010 FTF Guide mentions the term "whole-of-government" once, subsequent FTF program documents use the term more frequently.

[7]Several international agreements, including the *Paris Declaration on Aid Effectiveness*, the *Accra Agenda for Action*, and the *Five Rome Principles for Sustainable Global Food Security*, highlight the need for country ownership as a means to coordinate development efforts and achieve sustainability. At the country level, partners can engage in meaningful dialogue on a common framework for action, identify how resources align with strategic priorities, and determine how to address gaps and make adjustments. According to the FTF Guide, through FTF, the U.S. government is expanding its commitment to align investments with partner country priorities while also increasing its own transparency and accountability.

interviewed USAID and FTF partner agency officials in Washington, D.C.[8] We also assessed whether coordination was consistent with key practices for interagency collaboration.[9] To identify the extent to which USAID and U.S. FTF partner agency representatives believe that they were implementing a whole-of-government approach and country-led approach in planning and implementing FTF, we surveyed 499 USAID and U.S. FTF partner agency representatives implementing FTF in the 19 focus countries.[10] To identify the U.S. agency representatives implementing FTF, we obtained a list of all U.S. FTF representatives from USAID, and then confirmed with each agency the list of representatives in their agency who would meet our selection criteria. We administered the survey from May through August 2012. Overall, we achieved a weighted response rate of 72 percent, with 342 respondents to our survey.[11] Using information available to us for all survey recipients, such as employment

---

[8]In this report, FTF partner agencies include the Department of State, Millennium Challenge Corporation (MCC), Department of the Treasury (Treasury), Department of Agriculture (USDA), the Peace Corps, U.S. African Development Foundation (USADF) and the Overseas Private Investment Corporation (OPIC). We did not include the Department of Commerce and Office of the U.S. Trade Representative (USTR) because they have few representatives overseas who focus on FTF. However, some officials from the Departments of Commerce, Defense (DOD), and Health and Human Services (Centers for Disease Control, CDC) responded to our survey because USAID said they provided some support to FTF.

[9]GAO, *Results-Oriented Government: Practices That Can Help Enhance and Sustain Collaboration among Federal Agencies*, GAO-06-15 (Washington, D.C.: Oct. 21, 2005) and *Managing Results: Key Considerations for Implementing Interagency Collaborative Mechanisms*, GAO-12-1022 (Washington, D.C.: Sept. 27, 2012). To identify key practices, GAO reviewed academic literature and prior GAO and Congressional Research Service reports. In addition, GAO interviewed experts in coordination, collaboration, partnerships, and networks such as the National Academy of Public Administration. See GAO-06-15 and GAO-12-1022 for additional details.

[10]We sent a web-based survey to 551 USAID and FTF partner-country representatives but later determined 52 to be out of scope. After sending out the survey, we identified 52 key personnel who had left their post prior to our sending out the survey request, who told us that they did not work on FTF, who were U.S.-based, or who were otherwise out of scope. See app. I for additional information on the scope and methodology. See the e-supplement (GAO-13-815SP) for more information on the FTF survey questionnaire.

[11]We used Response Rate 3 (RR3) as defined by the American Association for Public Opinion Research in *Standard Definitions: Final Dispositions of Case Codes and Outcome Rates for Surveys*, 7th ed., 2011. Weighting accounts for the unequal agency sizes and response rates across agencies.

status, we conducted a nonresponse bias analysis.[12] The nonresponse bias analysis did not find any statistically measurable bias that would affect our analyses. Therefore, although our survey was intended to be a census, for the purposes of analyzing the results, we treat our survey as a random sample. Unless otherwise noted, point estimates we report for 2012 have a margin of error of no more than plus or minus 9 percentage points at the 95 percent level of confidence. We did not survey country stakeholders about the U.S. government country-led approach in the planning and implementation of FTF. To determine if USAID has identified risks with engaging key country stakeholders and documented efforts to mitigate them, two analysts independently reviewed, categorized, and analyzed USAID's 19 FTF multiyear country strategies. Appendix I contains additional information on our scope and methodology.

We conducted this performance audit from March 2013 to September 2013 in accordance with generally accepted government auditing standards. Those standards require that we plan and perform the audit to obtain sufficient, appropriate evidence to provide a reasonable basis for our findings and conclusions based on our audit objectives. We believe that the evidence obtained provides a reasonable basis for our findings and conclusions based on our audit objectives.

## Background

FTF is the U.S. government's global hunger and food security initiative. The overarching goal of the initiative is to accelerate progress toward the United Nation's Millennium Development Goal of halving the proportion of people living in extreme poverty and hunger by 2015. FTF pursues two paths toward this goal: (1) address the root causes of hunger that limit the potential of millions of people and (2) establish a lasting foundation for change by aligning resources with country-owned processes and sustained multistakeholder partnerships through a new country-led approach.[13] FTF also attempts to coordinate existing U.S. government programs in agriculture and food security through a whole-of-government

---

[12]A nonresponse bias analysis is used to verify that nonrespondents to the survey are not likely to answer differently from those who did respond and that the respondents are representative of the target population, thus ensuring that the results can be generalized to the population from which the sample was chosen.

[13]FTF also has a goal to reduce the prevalence of poverty and stunted children less than 5 years of age by 20 percent in the areas in which it works.

approach and complement the related work by multilateral institutions such as the World Bank that receive food security funds from the U.S. government.

The U.S. government selected 19 countries as focus countries for FTF on the basis of the level of need, opportunity for partnership, potential for agricultural-led growth, opportunity for regional synergies, and resource availability.[14] In these 19 countries, the U.S. government concentrates FTF investments in specific geographic regions called "zones of influence" where a small number of commodities such as rice, maize, and wheat are targeted.

In 2010, the Department of State and USAID's Quadrennial Diplomacy and Development Review (QDDR) designated USAID as the lead agency for the FTF initiative. USAID established the Bureau for Food Security to manage FTF as well as other agricultural development programs. Since that time, the USAID Administrator has served as the de facto Global Food Security Coordinator. In that capacity, he is responsible for implementing the initiative, including ensuring that all relevant U.S. government agencies and departments are consulted and engaged, as necessary, for the purposes of aligning and coordinating FTF with other food security-related programs and policies across the U.S. government. In addition, FTF has two Deputy Coordinators: one for development and one for diplomacy.[15]

To facilitate coordination of U.S. government activities at the country level, the U.S. ambassador in each focus country designates a U.S. FTF Country Coordinator to lead the whole-of-government implementation of FTF. The initiative incorporates USAID food security programs and activities of nine FTF partner agencies, as shown in table 1. Partner agency roles in implementing FTF include State's efforts to reform policy;

---

[14]The 19 FTF countries are Bangladesh, Cambodia, Ethiopia, Guatemala, Ghana, Haiti, Honduras, Kenya, Liberia, Malawi, Mali, Mozambique, Nepal, Rwanda, Senegal, Tajikistan, Tanzania, Uganda, and Zambia. In 2011, according to the FTF progress report, the U.S. government removed Nicaragua as a FTF country because the government of Nicaragua had not developed an effective country implementation plan that could guide U.S. investments, nor were its policies as conducive to success as other FTF focus countries.

[15]The Deputy Coordinator for Development is a position at USAID, and the Deputy Coordinator for Diplomacy is a position at State. The USAID Assistant to the Administrator for the Bureau for Food Security is also part of the leadership.

Treasury's support for the Global Agriculture and Food Security Program (GAFSP); and USDA's support for agricultural research, economic, and market analysis.[16]

**Table 1: U.S. Agency Roles in Implementing Feed the Future**

| Feed the Future (FTF) agency | FTF role |
| --- | --- |
| U.S. Agency for International Development (USAID) | is the lead agency that coordinates, implements, and assesses FTF programming at country and regional levels; directly programs agriculture, nutrition, and development food aid funding; and contributes to GAFSP. |
| Department of State (State) | is to use diplomatic means to improve coordination and increase global resources from other donors for agricultural investment, advance policy reforms that strengthen the effectiveness of agricultural investment, strengthen national frameworks for adoption of agricultural biotechnology, and partner with relevant UN agencies and other international organizations in pursuing the FTF agenda. |
| Millennium Challenge Corporation (MCC) | is to support country-led requests for agriculture and food security-related investments through MCC compacts including irrigation, roads, ports and post-harvest infrastructure, farmer training, agriculture finance, property rights, and land policy and nutrition. |
| Department of the Treasury (Treasury) | is to coordinate multilateral support for food security including contributions to the GAFSP, promote monitoring and evaluation of projects, leverage funding through a GAFSP private sector lending window, use influence to align multilateral development bank efforts with U.S. food security priorities, and oversee other multilateral development bank funding for agriculture. |
| Department of Agriculture (USDA) | is to support agricultural research and extension, data and economic analysis, market information and statistics, and in country capacity building. |
| Peace Corps | is responsible for community economic development, agriculture, environment, and nutrition. |
| U.S. African Development Foundation (USADF) | is to build the capacity of local farmers' associations and food processors in some African FTF countries. |
| Overseas Private Investment Corporation (OPIC) | is to support U.S. private sector investments in some FTF countries through insurance, debt financing, and support to private equity funds. |
| Department of Commerce | is to provide climate forecasting and guidance to some FTF countries on climate change mitigation and sustainable fisheries through the National Oceanic and Atmospheric Administration. |

---

[16]GAFSP is a multilateral donor trust fund to assist in the implementation of pledges made by the G20 countries, who asked the World Bank to establish such a fund to support the L'Aquila initiative to boost support for agriculture and food security. The objective of this trust fund is to address the underfunding of country and regional agriculture and food security strategic investment plans already being developed by countries in consultation with donors and other stakeholders at the country level. The United States has committed funds through GAFSP and coordinated the design and development of the new multilateral fund. As of March 2013, Treasury had disbursed $326 of the $475 million U.S. commitment. For specific information on agency food security programs and initiatives, see GAO-10-352.

| Feed the Future (FTF) agency | FTF role |
| --- | --- |
| U.S. Trade Representative (USTR) | is to advance work on trade and investment policy, including trade facilitation and other efforts to reduce barriers to efficient markets through Trade and Investment Framework Agreements. |

Source: USAID Feed the Future Progress Report, October 2012.

Together, USAID and the U.S. FTF partner agencies allocated $7 billion for global food security programs in fiscal years 2010 through 2013. As of March 2013, USAID and U.S. FTF partner agencies had disbursed approximately $4.5 billion, or about 63 percent (see table 2).[17]

---

[17]In 2012, USAID and State worked with a coalition of U.S.-based international relief and development organizations called InterAction to attract non-U.S.-government resources for FTF. InterAction has pledged more than $1 billion for food security and nutrition over 3 years.

GAO-13-809 Global Food Security

Table 2: Reported Annual Allocations and Disbursements for Feed the Future from Fiscal Year 2010 through March 31, 2013

Dollars in millions

| | FY 2010 | | FY 2011 | | FY 2012 | | FY 2013 (as of March 31, 2013) | | Total (2010-2013) | |
|---|---|---|---|---|---|---|---|---|---|---|
| | Allocated | Disbursed | Allocated | Disbursed | Allocated | Disbursed | Allocated | Disbursed | Allocated | Disbursed |
| **L'Aquila commitment** | | | | | | | | | 4,027.6 | 1,456.8 |
| USAID/State Feed the Future (FTF) | 808.6 | 595.9 | 943.4 | 379.2 | 953.6 | 100.5 | - | - | 2,705.5 | 1,075.5 |
| MCC: Agriculture and Food Security investments[a] | 739.4 | 0.0 | 241.5 | 12.0 | 0.01 | 32.4 | 0.1 | 10.5 | 981.1 | 54.8 |
| Treasury: GAFSP[b] | 66.6 | 66.6 | 124.8 | 99.8 | 149.6 | 160.0 | - | - | 341.0 | 326.4 |
| **Other FTF-related programs** | | | | | | | | | 3,016.3 | 3,015.6 |
| **USAID** | | | | | | | | | | |
| Nutrition (Global Health Programs) | 71.1 | 57.9 | 89.8 | 47.6 | 95.0 | 10.4 | - | - | 255.9 | 115.9 |
| Food for Peace Title II Development Food Aid | 385.5 | 385.5 | 422.6 | 422.6 | 426.8 | 426.8 | 331.0 | 56.6 | 1,566.0 | 1,291.6 |
| **MCC** | | | | | | | | | | |
| Food Security Investments[c] | 1.9 | 92.8 | 6.1 | 203.7 | 23.6 | 255.2 | 6.2 | 88.3 | 37.8 | 640.0 |
| **Treasury** | | | | | | | | | | |
| Treasury: International Fund for Agricultural Development | 30.0 | 30.0 | 29.4 | 29.4 | 30.0 | 30.0 | - | - | 89.4 | 89.4 |
| **USDA[d]** | | | | | | | | | | |
| Food for Progress | 106.7 | 81.8 | 183.7 | 74.2 | 239.9 | 128.2 | - | 147.1 | 530.3 | 431.4 |
| Local and Regional Procurement Pilot Project | 10.0 | 0.0 | 3.0 | 14.8 | 1.3 | 3.0 | - | 0.8 | 14.3 | 18.7 |
| McGovern-Dole Food for Education | 145.0 | 96.4 | 195.5 | 109.6 | 173.3 | 141.1 | - | 78.7 | 513.8 | 425.8 |
| Food Aid Nutrition Enhancement Program Competitive Grants Program | 2.7 | 1.5 | 0.0 | 0.0 | 0.0 | 0.0 | - | - | 2.7 | 1.5 |
| Cochran Fellowship Program | 0.3 | 0.0 | 0.1 | 0.0 | 1.5 | 0.3 | 1.8 | 0.3 | 3.8 | 0.6 |

GAO-13-809 Global Food Security

Dollars in millions

| | FY 2010 | | FY 2011 | | FY 2012 | | FY 2013 (as of March 31, 2013) | | Total (2010-2013) | |
|---|---|---|---|---|---|---|---|---|---|---|
| | Allocated | Disbursed | Allocated | Disbursed | Allocated | Disbursed | Allocated | Disbursed | Allocated | Disbursed |
| Norman E. Borlaug International Agricultural Science and Technology Fellowship Program | 0.2 | 0.0 | 0.3 | 0.1 | 1.7 | 0.2 | - | 0.4 | 2.2 | 0.7 |
| **Totals** | | | | | | | | | **7,043.9** | **4,472.3** |

Legend: FY = fiscal year; State = Department of State; USAID = U.S. Agency for International Development; MCC = Millennium Challenge Corporation; Treasury= Department of the Treasury; GAFSP = Global Agriculture and Food Security Program; USDA = U.S. Department of Agriculture.

Source: GAO analysis of agency data.

Notes: Columns may not sum to totals due to rounding. The information reported as allocations and disbursements was provided to us by the agencies. We use the term "allocations" to refer to funds the agencies reported that they directed to FTF. We did not independently assess the amounts agencies reported as allocations and disbursements. USAID/State includes funding for the 19 FTF focus countries, nine regional bureaus, 33 aligned countries, three strategic partner countries, the Bureau for Food Security, and other USAID departments such as the Economic Growth Agriculture and Trade Office. USAID/State, Treasury, and USDA annual disbursements for fiscal years 2010, 2011, and 2012 reflect disbursements to date (as of March 31, 2013) against funds allocated for each year. As of March 31, 2013, fiscal year 2013 funding for State and Foreign Operations had not been appropriated. MCC disbursements reflect disbursements made in that given year. MCC data include new agreements that entered into force in fiscal years 2010 through 2012. Funding for the Peace Corps, the U.S. African Development Foundation (USADF), the U.S. Trade Representative (USTR), the Department of Commerce (Commerce), and the Overseas Private Investment Corporation (OPIC) are not tracked or reported for FTF purposes. USAID officials noted, however, that the Peace Corps and USADF plan to provide FTF funding data to USAID in fiscal year 2013. According to USAID, Commerce and USTR do not receive specific food security funding; they provide support and technical expertise to FTF. OPIC did not receive FTF funding during this period. For a description of the other FTF-related programs, see appendix II.

[a] MCC funding is no-year funding. MCC's allocations and disbursements are tracked against the fiscal year in which the transaction is recorded. MCC's compacts are active for 5 years. Allocations take place upon compact signing and program reallocation of the budget within that compact can take place during the 5- year life of the compact. Disbursements take place anytime during the 5-year window of the compact lifecycle.

[b] According to USAID and State, State and USAID funding was transferred to Treasury for the U.S. contribution to the GAFSP: $66.6 million in fiscal year 2010, $25 million in fiscal year 2011, and $14.6 million in fiscal year 2012. According to USAID officials, all transfers in fiscal year 2011 and fiscal year 2012 were to the GAFSP's Private Sector Window.

[c] MCC funding data shown are for the following agricultural components of these compacts that entered into force prior to fiscal year 2010: Burkina Faso, Mongolia, Morocco, Mozambique, Namibia, and Tanzania. According to MCC, the majority of food security allocations were made at the point of entry into force of each compact, which was prior to the fiscal years shown in table 2.

[d] The agency reported that food assistance programs are multi-year programs and the funds are drawdown gradually. According to USDA, due to the March 31st 2013 cutoff, funds were yet to be allocated for the fiscal year 2013 food assistance programs.

GAO-13-809 Global Food Security

Of this amount, disbursements against the L'Aquila pledge accounted for $1.5 billion or about 33 percent, while other FTF-related programs were $3 billion or 67 percent.

[18] Within other FTF-related programs, USAID disbursed the highest amount of funds ($1.4 billion), followed by USDA ($879 million), MCC ($640 million) and Treasury ($89 million).

Figure 1 shows USAID and U.S. FTF partner agency locations in the 19 FTF focus countries in 2012. USAID and State have representatives in all 19 countries, while MCC, USADF, and the Peace Corps are located in countries where they have food security programs, and USDA predominantly operates on a regional level. The countries with the highest number of FTF agencies are Mali, Senegal, and Tanzania while the countries with the lowest number of FTF agencies are Bangladesh, Haiti, Honduras, and Tajikistan.

---

[18]See app. II for a description of the other FTF-related food security programs implemented by USAID, Treasury, and USDA.

**Figure 1: Map of USAID and Feed the Future (FTF) Partner Agency Representatives in the 19 FTF Countries, in 2012**

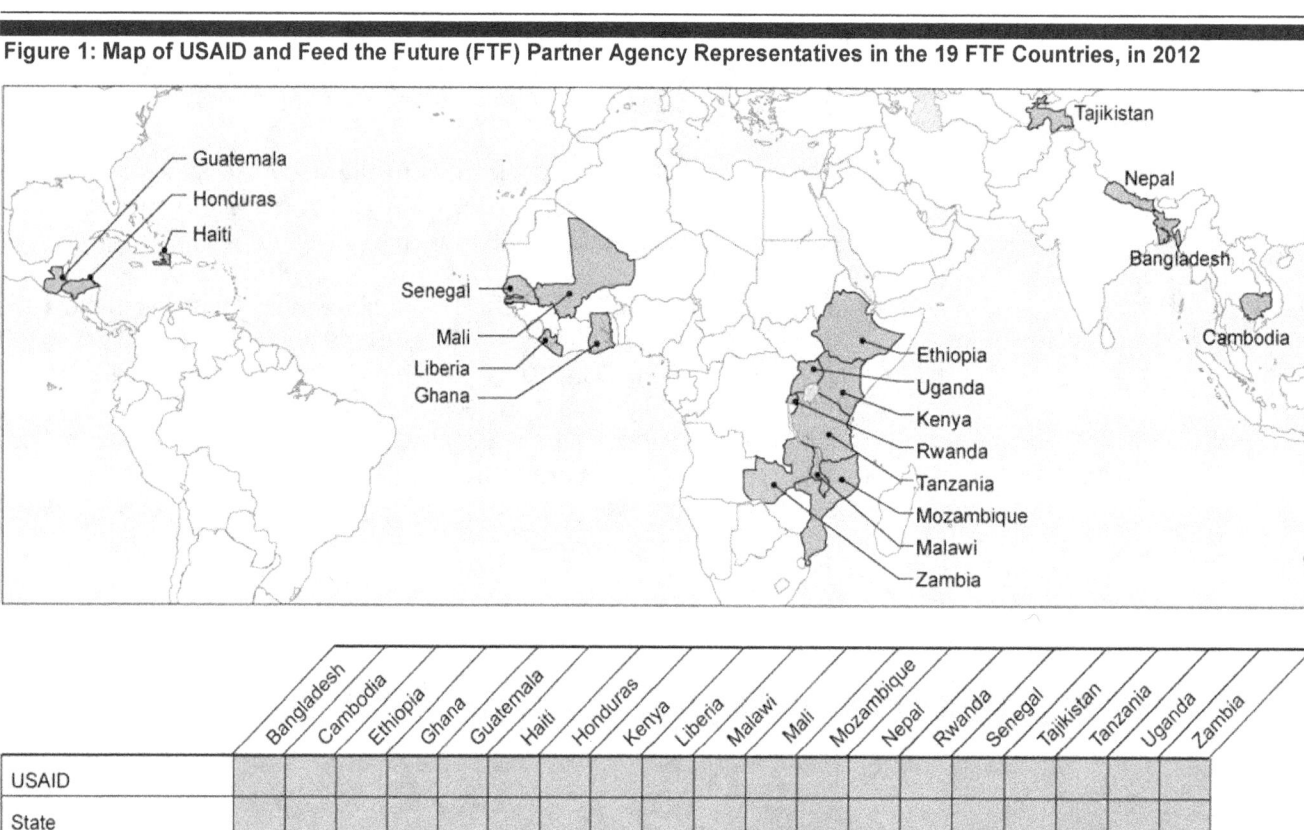

| | Bangladesh | Cambodia | Ethiopia | Ghana | Guatemala | Haiti | Honduras | Kenya | Liberia | Malawi | Mali | Mozambique | Nepal | Rwanda | Senegal | Tajikistan | Tanzania | Uganda | Zambia |
|---|---|---|---|---|---|---|---|---|---|---|---|---|---|---|---|---|---|---|---|
| USAID | ▒ | ▒ | ▒ | ▒ | ▒ | ▒ | ▒ | ▒ | ▒ | ▒ | ▒ | ▒ | ▒ | ▒ | ▒ | ▒ | ▒ | ▒ | ▒ |
| State | ▒ | ▒ | ▒ | ▒ | ▒ | ▒ | ▒ | ▒ | ▒ | ▒ | ▒ | ▒ | ▒ | ▒ | ▒ | ▒ | ▒ | ▒ | ▒ |
| MCC | | | ▒ | ▒ | | | ▒ | | | ▒ | ▒ | ▒ | | | ▒ | | ▒ | | ▒ |
| USADF | | | | | | | ▒ | ▒ | ▒ | ▒ | | | | ▒ | ▒ | | ▒ | | |
| Peace Corps | | ▒ | ▒ | ▒ | ▒ | | | ▒ | ▒ | ▒ | ▒ | ▒ | ▒ | ▒ | ▒ | | ▒ | ▒ | ▒ |
| USDA regional presence[a] | ○ | ○ | ◉ | ○ | ◉ | ○ | ○ | ◉ | ○ | ○ | ○ | ○ | ○ | ○ | ◉ | ○ | ○ | ○ | ○ |

▒ In-country ..... (Agency bilateral presence)

◉ .................... (USDA regional representative is based in the country)

○ .................... (USDA representative is based in another country)

MCC Millennium Challenge Corporation
State Department of State
USADF United States African Development Foundation
USAID United States Agency for International Development
USDA United States Department of Agriculture

Source: GAO analysis from agency data. Map Resources (map).

Note: The FTF partners listed had specific FTF programmatic activity in the focus countries in 2012.

[a] For those countries in which the U.S. Department of Agriculture (USDA) regional representative is based in another country, USDA covers these countries as follows: Bangladesh and Nepal are covered from India; Cambodia is covered from Thailand; Ghana and Liberia are covered from Nigeria; Haiti is covered from the Dominican Republic; Honduras is covered from Guatemala; Malawi,

Rwanda, Tanzania, Uganda, and Zambia are covered from Kenya; Mali is covered from Senegal; Mozambique is covered from South Africa; and Tajikistan is covered from Turkey.

# USAID Has Made Progress in Coordinating with U.S. FTF Partner Agencies through Its Whole-of-Government Approach

USAID has made progress in applying FTF's whole-of-government approach by coordinating and integrating U.S. FTF partner agencies' knowledge and expertise at three levels: at headquarters in Washington, D.C.; in each of the 19 FTF focus countries; and between the countries and headquarters. At the headquarters level, we found USAID has made significant progress in addressing vulnerabilities we previously reported on by coordinating with U.S. FTF partner agencies to, among other things, develop a global food security strategy and monitor interagency performance. In addition, USAID and U.S. FTF partner agency representatives reported coordinating with each other at the country level and between the countries and headquarters. For example, our survey of U.S. FTF representatives in 19 FTF focus countries shows that 93 percent of the U.S. FTF partner agency representatives reported coordinating with USAID and approximately 80 percent of all U.S. FTF representatives reported coordinating with their headquarters office. Figure 2 illustrates USAID's whole-of-government coordination efforts in headquarters, at the country level, and between the country level and headquarters.

**Figure 2: USAID-Led Whole-of-Government Approach to the Feed the Future (FTF) Initiative**

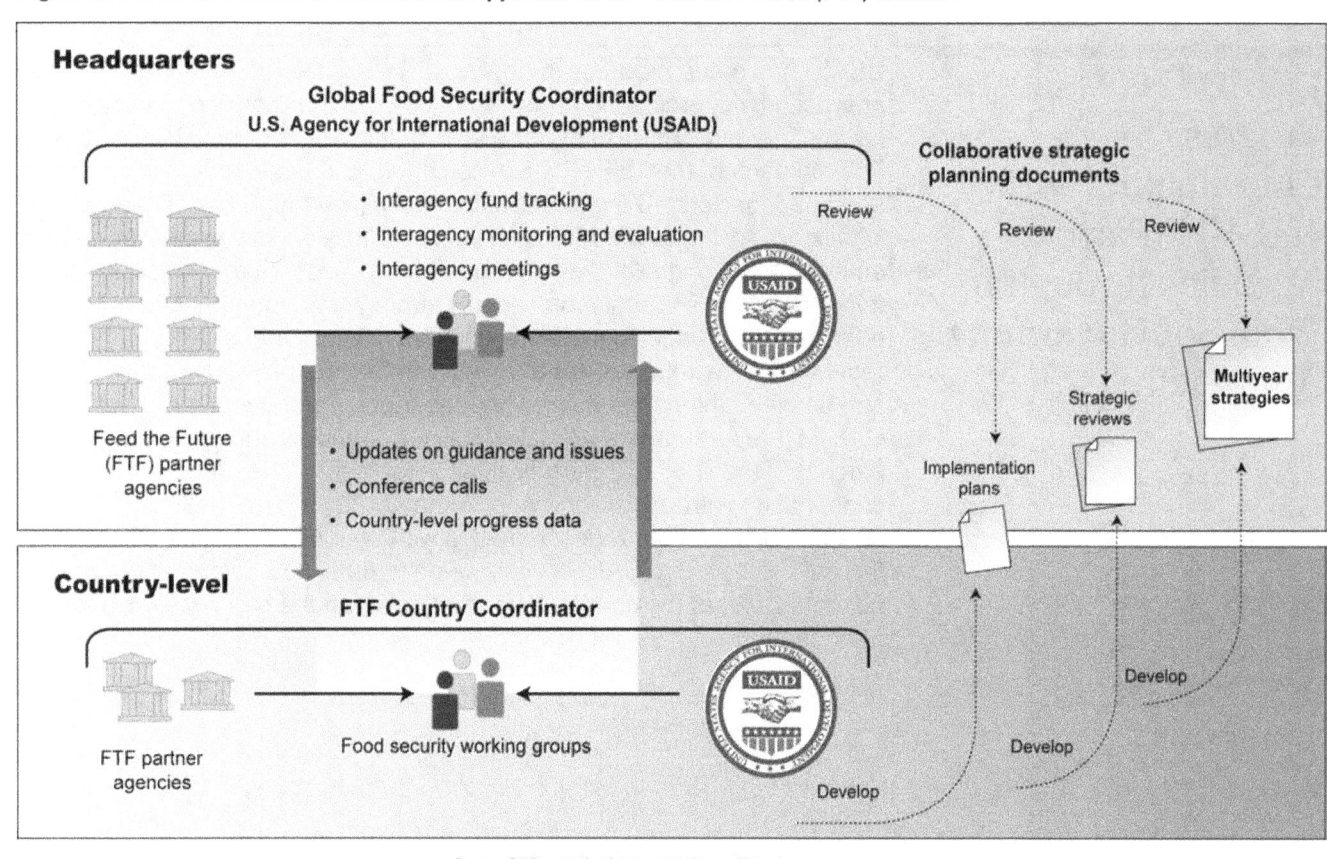

Source: GAO analysis of documentation and interviews.

Note: Country-level activities occur within each of the 19 FTF countries.

## USAID Has Made Significant Progress in Coordinating with FTF Partners in Headquarters

Since 2010, USAID has made significant progress in addressing fragmentation in global food security efforts by coordinating with FTF partner agencies in headquarters through FTF's whole-of-government approach. In reports issued in 2008 and 2010, we found that vulnerabilities in U.S. food security efforts included the lack of government-wide efforts such as an integrated strategy for food security, data management systems, and leveraging knowledge and expertise through coordination efforts such as food security working groups.[19] Most of these vulnerabilities were related to a lack of coordination among U.S. agencies at the headquarters level. We concluded that, given this fragmentation in food security, the U.S. government was likely missing opportunities to leverage each agency's expertise and to minimize duplication. We made several recommendations on improving coordination efforts in food security programs. U.S. agencies agreed with our recommendations and said they would take actions to develop an interagency food security strategy and establish a common reporting system to monitor progress in food security programs.

As a result, USAID has made significant progress in coordinating food security programs at the headquarters level by (1) developing a strategic approach to food security in collaboration with other U.S. agencies, (2) tracking interagency food security funding, (3) tracking and monitoring interagency food security performance data, and (4) coordinating food security efforts through biweekly interagency meetings. These efforts are consistent with key practices that enhance interagency collaboration.[20]

## FTF Strategy Documents Represent Progress toward a Government-wide Global Food Security Strategy

Since 2010, U.S. agencies have made progress in outlining their joint strategic approach for global food security programs in various documents. The 2010 Feed the Future Guide (FTF Guide) —the strategic document guiding FTF—states that the overarching FTF goal is sustainably reducing poverty and hunger by tackling their root causes and employing proven strategies for achieving large scale and lasting impact. The FTF Guide also indentifies increasing agricultural growth and improving nutritional status of women and children as two key objectives to achieve progress towards the overarching goal. The outlining of a joint

---

[19]See GAO, *International Food Security: Insufficient Efforts by Host Governments and Donors Threaten Progress to Halve Hunger in Sub-Saharan Africa by 2015*, GAO-08-680 (Washington, D.C.: May 29, 2008); and *Global Food Security: U.S. Agencies Progressing on Governmentwide Strategy, but Approach Faces Several Vulnerabilities*, GAO-10-352 (Washington, D.C.: Mar. 11, 2010).

[20]GAO, *Results-Oriented Government: Practices That Can Help Enhance and Sustain Collaboration among Federal Agencies*, GAO-06-15 (Washington, D.C.: Oct. 21, 2005). For the purpose of this report, we use the term "collaboration" broadly to include interagency activities that others have variously defined as "cooperation," "coordination," "integration," or "networking." We have done so because there are no commonly accepted definitions for these terms, and we are unable to make definitive distinctions between these different types of interagency activities. We define collaboration as any joint activity by two or more organizations that is intended to produce more public value than could be produced when the organizations act alone (see GAO-06-15).

strategic approach for FTF is consistent with our previous recommendation that agencies develop a comprehensive global food security strategy. The FTF Guide specifies that U.S. agencies involved in food-security-related activities are to participate in planning and implementing the initiative. FTF officials told us that the U.S. agencies primarily involved in food security—USAID, State, USDA, MCC, and Treasury—collaborated on the development of the FTF Guide. The 2012 Feed the Future Progress Report, issued after the FTF Guide, provides additional information such as U.S. agency roles and responsibilities in implementing the U.S. government strategic approach. USAID officials told us they are updating the FTF Guide to include roles and responsibilities. These efforts are consistent with one of our key practices on interagency collaboration, which notes that in order for collaborating agencies to achieve a common outcome, they need to establish strategies that work together with their partners' strategies or are developed as joint strategies.[21]

### USAID Created Budget Director Position to Track Interagency FTF Funding

USAID also made progress in tracking interagency funding by establishing the position of FTF Budget Director who requests and tracks funding data on U.S. global food security programs. Consistent with our previous recommendation that agencies periodically inventory food security-related programs and funding, the FTF Budget Director requests quarterly data from USAID, MCC, and Treasury on appropriations, obligations, and disbursements toward the L'Aquila pledge. The Budget Director also tracks appropriated funds for other food security programs such as USDA's Food for Progress and Food for Education programs and Treasury's contributions toward the International Fund for Agricultural Development by requesting data semiannually. The funding data collected are reported in USAID's annual Feed the Future Progress Report.

### USAID Has Begun to Track Interagency Performance Data Using an FTF Monitoring and Evaluation System

USAID has also made progress in establishing an FTF monitoring and evaluation system to track interagency performance data toward common future security goals using a shared online data input and reporting system. We previously recommended that agencies develop improved measures to monitor and evaluate progress.[22] USAID and the FTF

---

[21]GAO-06-15.

[22]GAO, *International Food Security: Insufficient Efforts by Host Governments and Donors Threaten Progress to Halve Hunger in Sub-Saharan Africa by 2015*, GAO-08-680 (Washington, D.C.: May 29, 2008).

partner agencies agreed on this centralized system and common indicators for tracking food security programs and progress across agencies. According to U.S. officials, USAID, State, USDA, MCC, Treasury, OPIC, and the Office of Management and Budget (OMB) collaborated on developing 56 FTF performance indicators for monitoring and evaluation, including 8 indicators that show U.S. government progress toward meeting FTF goals. These indicators include prevalence of poverty and prevalence of underweight children under 5 years of age. However, initially not all U.S. FTF partner agencies reported into the FTF Monitoring System (FTFMS) that USAID established. In fiscal year 2011, USAID, USDA, MCC, and Treasury reported on these indicators. The Peace Corps began reporting into the system in 2012, and USADF began reporting into the system in fiscal year 2013. OPIC officials told us that they plan to report into the system in 2014.[23]

USAID uses data from FTFMS to report on the implementation of its whole-of-government and country-led approaches in the FTF Scorecard—which includes, among other things, measures to track the whole-of-government approach. According to the FTF Scorecard, USAID is tracking five whole-of-government related measures including the number of FTF interagency biweekly meetings and agencies presenting their food security annual plans to FTF. This is consistent with another of our key practices for interagency collaboration: that collaborating agencies create the means to monitor and evaluate those efforts so that they can identify areas for improvement and report to clients and stakeholders.[24] In fiscal year 2012, of the five whole-of-government measures, results reported in the FTF Scorecard

- *exceeded the target for one*: number of partner agencies reporting into FTFMS;
- *partially met the target for three*: number of FTF interagency working group meetings, number of country-level working groups holding regular interagency meetings, number of FTF agencies presenting their food security annual plans to FTF; and

---

[23]According to USAID officials, State, Commerce, and USTR do not have in country food security programs, and thus do not report into the FTFMS.

[24]GAO-06-15.

- *did not meet the target for one*: number of country portfolio reviews with interagency participation.[25]

## USAID and FTF Partner Agencies Hold Biweekly Meetings to Coordinate at Headquarters

Since 2010, USAID and FTF partner agencies have shared expertise and knowledge through biweekly headquarters meetings that all the FTF partner agencies we spoke with confirmed attending. In May 2008, we found that agencies did not have a government-wide interagency working group to coordinate their food security programs.[26] On the basis of our current review of interagency meeting agendas and notes, we found USAID and FTF partners discussed planning documents such as the FTF strategic plan and progress reports and coordinated USAID and FTF partner agency feedback on the documents. FTF officials also told us that at these interagency meetings, agencies share implementation plans, discuss FTF plans and documents, request input, raise and discuss issues regarding implementation, and present information on their areas of expertise. This is consistent with our key practices for federal agencies engaged in collaborative efforts, which state that collaborating agencies create the means to address the compatibility of policies and procedures and other means to facilitate working across agency boundaries such as frequent communication among collaborating agencies.[27]

## USAID and U.S. FTF Partners Reported Coordination at the Country Level and between the Country Level and Headquarters

USAID and U.S. FTF partner agency representatives we surveyed in 19 FTF countries reported coordination at the country level and between the country level and headquarters through USAID's whole-of-government approach.

---

[25]In fiscal year 2012, the results and targets for each of the five measures were reported as: number of partner agencies reporting into FTFMS (5 of 4), number of FTF interagency working group meetings (19 of 24), country-level working groups holding regular interagency meetings (15 of 19), agencies presenting their food security annual plans to FTF (3 of 4), and country portfolio reviews with interagency participation (0 of 6).

[26]GAO-08-680.

[27]GAO-06-15 and see GAO, *Key Considerations for Implementing Interagency Collaborative Mechanisms*, GAO-12-1022 (Washington, D.C.: Sept. 27, 2012).

Coordination at the Country Level

At the country level, 93 percent of U.S. FTF partner agency representatives reported coordinating with representatives from the lead FTF organization, USAID, in planning and implementing FTF. Approximately 66 percent of representatives from U.S. FTF partner agencies also reported coordinating with country-level FTF representatives from State, and approximately one-third or more of U.S. FTF partner agency representatives reported coordinating with USDA, the Peace Corps, and other FTF agency representatives (see table 3).[28]

**Table 3: Percentage of U.S. Agency Representatives in 19 Feed the Future (FTF) Countries Who Reported Coordination with Country-Level Representatives from Other Agencies in Planning and Implementing FTF**

| Respondent group | Percentage reporting coordination with | | | | |
|---|---|---|---|---|---|
| | USAID | State | USDA | Peace Corps | Other[a] |
| FTF partner agencies | 93 | 66 | 35 | 39 | 41 |
| U.S. Agency for International Development (USAID) | - | 60 | 52 | 40 | 40 |

Legend: State = Department of State; USDA = U.S. Department of Agriculture.

Source: GAO survey.

Notes: All point estimates have a margin of error of no more than plus or minus 9 percentage points.

[a]The "Other" category includes the Departments of Commerce and the Treasury, the Millennium Challenge Corporation, and the U.S. African Development Foundation.

We undertook additional analysis of the coordination reported in the survey and found that in nearly all cases USAID's coordination with its partner agencies was a two-way relationship.[29] For example, USAID officials reported coordinating with State, MCC, Treasury, USDA, the Peace Corps, and Commerce in all countries where those agencies were involved in FTF. Those same agencies also reported coordinating with USAID in all the FTF countries where they were present. We also found that a broad range of USAID representatives reported coordinating with FTF partner agency staff, including mission directors, Foreign Service Officers, personal services contractors, and Foreign Service Nationals. The USAID staff in our survey indicated that they worked in areas such as agricultural development, economic growth, food security, and health.[30]

---

[28]U.S. agencies have not established criteria for an optimal level of coordination.

[29]We looked at USAID's coordination with its partner agencies in all of the 19 FTF countries where the partner agencies had at least one representative that responded to the survey.

[30]See the e-supplement (GAO-13-815SP) for more information on the FTF survey questionnaire.

Collectively, USAID representatives reported coordinating with multiple officials at the State, USDA, and the Peace Corps. For example USAID coordinated with U.S. ambassadors, political and economic affairs officers, and public affairs officers at State.[31]

Within each FTF country, USAID coordinates and shares knowledge and expertise with FTF partner agencies, under the leadership of the FTF Country Coordinator, through food security working groups as well as informal communication.[32] Almost 80 percent of FTF partner representatives reported coordinating with USAID in FTF meetings at least quarterly. USAID FTF country-level representatives we interviewed while they were in Washington, D.C., told us that the interagency meetings in the field are their formal means of coordination. According to USAID documents, all FTF country-level staff report meeting at least twice a year; however, the frequency of these FTF meetings and the topics covered vary from country to country. For example, FTF officials in one Asian country told us that their food security working group meets once a week and discusses topics such as FTF and other food security-related projects, document development, budgets, and stakeholder meetings. By contrast, officials in an African country told us that FTF partner agencies meet quarterly to discuss FTF issues and implementation but certain agencies meet more frequently as needed and during development of FTF documents. According to senior USAID officials in headquarters, they have suggested to country-level staff that they hold interagency meetings at least monthly, but USAID has no requirement regarding the frequency of the meetings.

Most USAID and partner agency representatives responding to our survey indicated that their coordination was generally effective in accomplishing a number of FTF-related actions,[33] as shown in table 4.

---

[31]See app. III for an illustrative example of U.S. representatives' reported coordination with FTF partner agencies in one country.

[32]The FTF Country Coordinator is typically the USAID Mission Director.

[33]We also used these survey results to examine the impact of various factors on the U.S. representatives' perceptions of whether their coordination had been effective in accomplishing the actions listed in table 4. For details on that multiple regression analysis, see app. IV.

**Table 4: Percentage of USAID and Feed the Future (FTF) Partner Agency Representatives Who Reported Their Coordination with All Other Partners Was Generally Effective in Accomplishing Certain Actions**

| Type of FTF action | Percentage reporting generally effective[a] | | |
| --- | --- | --- | --- |
| | All | USAID | FTF partner agencies |
| Developing/contributing to integrated FTF program documents | 76 | 77 | 74 |
| Integrating FTF program/project planning with other US foreign assistance programs | 72 | 73 | 70 |
| Sharing observations/information obtained through meetings with other stakeholders | 69 | 73 | 59 |
| Sharing observations/information obtained through meetings with host government officials | 68 | 71 | 59 |
| Identifying donors/partners | 62 | 63 | 58 |
| Developing joint/compatible procedures/processes for FTF activities | 60 | 60 | 60 |
| Developing joint communication plans, reports and/or cables | 56 | 57 | 53 |

Source: GAO survey.

Notes: For "All" and "USAID" responses, the point estimates have a margin of error of no more than plus or minus 3 percentage points. For "FTF partner agencies" responses, the point estimates have a margin of error of no more than plus or minus 7 percentage points. There were other responses that included "no opinion" and "not effective." The "not effective" responses, not shown in this table, were all under 8 percent for these actions. We presented those actions that focused on interagency coordination. For the full list of actions, see the Q33 series in the e-supplement (GAO-13-815SP).

[a]We grouped responses for "very" and "somewhat effective."

About three out of four FTF agency representatives (76 percent) indicated that their coordination was generally effective in developing or contributing to integrated FTF program documents, and our review of agency documents identified multiple examples of such efforts. USAID and USDA, for example, jointly prepared a roadmap to align their food assistance programs with FTF as part of the multiyear strategy development process in Guatemala and Haiti. Seventy-two percent of USAID and U.S. FTF partner agency representatives also reported generally effective coordination in integrating FTF program or project planning with other U.S. foreign assistance programs.

Over half of U.S. FTF representatives responding to our survey indicated that certain factors helped interagency coordination at the country level, such as ongoing communication (65 percent), sharing FTF-related data (64 percent), and the technical expertise of other U.S. government staff (61 percent). Less than half of all U.S. FTF representatives indicated that certain factors either hindered coordination or had no effect, such as staffing levels at other agencies (34 percent), lack of compatibility of procedures (39 percent), and flexibility of funding (41 percent).[34]

## Coordination between Country Level and Headquarters

Between the country level and headquarters, USAID and FTF partners reported coordinating and sharing information with each other through a variety of methods, including written communications and guidance, review of country strategies and progress data, country visits, and conference calls. Approximately 80 percent of USAID and U.S. FTF partner agency representatives reported coordinating with their offices in headquarters on FTF. About 90 percent of all USAID representatives reported coordinating with USAID's Bureau for Food Security on FTF. In addition, 73 percent of USAID and U.S. FTF partner agencies reported that they received FTF guidance from their own headquarters at least quarterly. All FTF agencies in headquarters provided written guidance to country-level staff on implementing FTF and requested updates on food security issues. Headquarters and country-level staff within USAID and FTF partner agencies also coordinated in the development and review of a series of FTF country strategic documents and progress data reported into the FTF monitoring and evaluation system.[35] Moreover, headquarters officials from USAID, USDA, and the Peace Corps also told us that they hold regular telephone conferences with country-level staff.

---

[34]This question in the GAO survey asked about factors that helped, hindered, or had no effect on respondents' coordination with all in-country U.S. government representatives to plan or implement FTF-related activities.

[35]In 2010, country-level staff in each FTF country developed a plan outlining the U.S. government approach for the first year of FTF implementation as well as a new multiyear strategy for implementing FTF. Headquarters staff reviewed the plans and strategies. Reviewers included the *de facto* Global Food Security Coordinator, deputy coordinators, Bureau of Food Security, and representatives from State, Commerce, MCC, USDA, OPIC, and the Peace Corps. These reviewers provided their evaluation and feedback to the country-level staff, drawing from each reviewer's agency expertise. For example, officials recommended to USAID staff in one Latin American country that their strategy elaborate on the alignment of FTF with interagency partners by clearly delineating partner roles in achieving FTF objectives. In 2011 and 2012, staff in each country revised their drafts of the implementation plan and multiyear strategy to incorporate the interagency input from the reviews and finalize their multiyear strategy. The final FTF multiyear strategies outline the 5-year strategic planning for FTF within each country and include agriculture and nutrition objectives, monitoring and evaluation plans, and interagency financial planning.

## USAID Facilitated a Country-Led Approach and Made Some Progress in Monitoring Risks but Has Not Systematically Assessed Risks at the Country Level

USAID has taken steps to facilitate a country-led approach by providing support to the development and implementation of each country's food security plan and by coordinating with multiple stakeholders. We found that USAID has a performance management tool, the FTF Scorecard, that is monitoring some risks to the country-led approach and that USAID has efforts to mitigate some of those risks. However, FTF's multiyear country strategies did not systematically assess risks to the country-led approach and identify mitigation plans. USAID did not require a risk assessment in its FTF strategy guidance; however, other relevant USAID guidance states that a risk assessment informs management of the relevant risks associated with achieving objectives.

### USAID Has Taken Steps to Facilitate a Country-Led Approach

We found that USAID has taken steps to facilitate a country-led approach. According to the FTF Guide, the country-led approach to FTF involves (1) providing support to the development and implementation of each country's food security plan, called a country investment plan (CIP) and (2) coordinating with multiple stakeholders, including the host government, civil society organizations, donors, and the private sector in the planning and implementation of FTF.[36] The U.S. government also planned to align its own multiyear country strategies with the priorities identified in the CIPs.

---

[36]The U.S. government's country-led approach to implementing global food security is outlined in the FTF Guide, the *Presidential Policy Directive on Global Development*, and the *Quadrennial Diplomacy and Development Review*. The FTF Guide states that the U.S. government will be guided by the *Five Rome Principles for Sustainable Global Food Security*, which the United States and 192 other countries unanimously endorsed in 2009. These principles reflect a concerted global effort to accelerate progress toward the UN Millennium Development Goal of halving the proportion of people living in extreme poverty and hunger by 2015. Two principles relate to country ownership in support of food security programs. These principles call on governments to, among other things, consult with a broad group of stakeholders in planning and implementing food security programs.

## USAID Supported Development and Implementation of Country Plans

We found that USAID and FTF partner agencies provided support to the development and implementation of CIPs in several ways. According to USAID officials, consistent with the FTF Guide, they provided support to the CIP development and implementation process through (1) assistance to strengthen the capacity of host governments and facilitate their consultation with multiple stakeholders; (2) financial and technical support to increase stakeholders' influence in developing and implementing the plans; and (3) participation in technical reviews of country investment plans to ensure, among other things, that the CIP development process, which included host government consultations with stakeholders, was carried out.[37]

In our survey of U.S. agency representatives in 19 FTF focus countries, USAID representatives reported that USAID provided multiple types of assistance to strengthen the capacity of host governments and to support host government officials' consultations with other stakeholders, including technical assistance or research data (71 percent), meetings (70 percent), and directly hosting consultation events or activities (68 percent). Sixty-two percent also reported providing policy or diplomatic support to improve host country laws, regulations, or organizational procedures relating to stakeholder consultations. In addition, over half of USAID representatives responding to the survey reported that, as a result of their coordination with host government stakeholders, partnership formation and engagement with other FTF project partners increased.

Our survey also showed that USAID representatives reported that they provided support to increase stakeholders' involvement in developing and implementing the country plans. For example, more than half of USAID representatives reported identifying potential partners and about half reported providing technical assistance or research data to for-profit stakeholders to facilitate the creation of public-private partnerships. In addition, half of USAID respondents reported that, as a result of their coordination with for-profit stakeholders, partnership formation with these stakeholders increased. Table 5 shows the percentages of USAID

---

[37]Other support included studies or modeling to improve the evidence informing decisions on food security priorities and financial expertise to develop estimates on the costs of financing the priorities outlined in the CIP.

representatives who indicated that USAID provided assistance to for-profit stakeholders to facilitate FTF-related public-private partnerships.[38]

**Table 5: Percentage of USAID Representatives Who Reported Feed the Future (FTF) Assistance USAID Provided to For-Profit Stakeholders to Facilitate Public-Private Partnerships, by Type of Assistance**

| Type of assistance | Percentage reporting USAID provided |
| --- | --- |
| Identified potential partners | 59 |
| Technical assistance or research data to facilitate the creation of public-private partnerships | 52 |
| Directly hosted an event or activity to facilitate partnership creation | 49 |
| Funded partnerships for this type of stakeholder | 44 |
| Funding to build capacity of this stakeholder to enter into a public-private partnership | 37 |

Source: GAO survey

Note: All point estimates have a margin of error of no more than plus or minus 4 percentage points.

USAID and U.S. FTF partner agency officials also participated in technical reviews of CIPs in all FTF focus countries, but the process for the reviews varied. For the African FTF focus countries, USAID relied on the African Union's Comprehensive Africa Agriculture Development Program (CAADP) to guide the development and implementation of country investment plans.[39] CAADP's framework requires a technical review of CIPs, which includes reviewing the prioritization of agriculture investments, documentation of the scope and form of stakeholder consultations in the planning process, incorporation of private sector investment, and a risk assessment.[40] For the non-African FTF focus countries, USAID and MCC officials told us that they and State promoted guidelines similar to CAADP and provided support for technical reviews

---

[38]Public-private partnerships are those between government agencies and either for-profit or nonprofit organizations.

[39]CAADP is an Africa-wide framework for developing, implementing, and measuring agriculture development investments at national, regional, and continent levels.

[40]The CAADP regional process requires, among other things, that the host government develop its CIP with the participation of civil society and private sector stakeholders; that the CIPs undergo a technical review; and that donors, the host government, and representatives of the private sector and civil society convene a business meeting to endorse the CIP and commit to its implementation. During implementation of its CIP, CAADP requires a country to conduct a multistakeholder review, called a joint sector review, to assess the performance and results of the agriculture sector.

because such a regional-level program to guide the development and implementation of the CIPs did not exist.

## U.S. FTF Agency Representatives Reported Coordination with Multiple Stakeholders

In our survey of U.S. FTF agency representatives in the 19 FTF focus countries, USAID and partner agency representatives reported that multiple stakeholders were included in the planning and implementation of FTF: host governments, nonprofit organizations, donors, and for-profit entities.[41] U.S. government officials seek to coordinate with host government, nonprofit, donor, and private sector stakeholders to implement FTF as follows:

- **Host government**: U.S. government officials are to coordinate with host governments on implementing agriculture policy reforms and consult with them on FTF policy priorities and investments.
- **Nonprofits**: U.S. government officials are to coordinate with nonprofits to build their capacity and to achieve meaningful and effective engagement with host governments to sustain food security investments.
- **Donors**: USAID is to participate in agriculture donor working groups in FTF countries to coordinate U.S. government food security investments with those of other donors. Additionally, one of State's roles is to encourage other donors to, among other things, meet their financial commitments to food security and to assist countries on policy reforms.
- **For-profits**: USAID is trying to increase private sector investment in agriculture in FTF focus countries, including through public-private partnerships.

As shown in table 6, the percentages of all U.S. FTF agency representatives that reported working with the four kinds of stakeholders ranged from 83 percent (working with host government officials) to 62 percent (working with for-profit enterprises).

---

[41]In our survey, stakeholders are those who are affected by a development outcome or have an interest in a development outcome.

**Table 6: Percentage of U.S. Agency Feed the Future (FTF) Representatives Who Reported Working with Stakeholders on FTF Planning and Implementation, by Stakeholder Type**

| Respondent group | Percentage reporting working with | | | |
| --- | --- | --- | --- | --- |
| | Host government officials | Nonprofits | Donors | For-profits |
| All | 83 | 74 | 63 | 62 |
| USAID | 86 | 79 | 73 | 68 |
| U.S. FTF partner agencies | 76 | 58 | 37 | 45 |

Legend: USAID = U.S. Agency for International Development.
Source: GAO survey.

Notes: For "All" and "USAID" responses, the point estimates have a margin of error of no more than plus or minus 4 percentage points. For "U.S. FTF partner agencies" responses, the point estimates have a margin of error of no more than plus or minus 7 percentage points.

Compared with representatives from U.S. FTF partner agencies, USAID representatives had a higher percentage reporting that they worked with each of the four stakeholder groups. As the lead agency for FTF, USAID engages a broad range of stakeholders, while FTF partner agencies may work with only certain groups of stakeholders depending on an agency's role in a focus country's FTF effort. For example, MCC works directly with host governments to design MCC compacts and support their implementation. In contrast, USADF provides grants directly to local organizations to fund projects that engage community groups in the design and implementation of the projects. (See app. V for additional information on agencies' country-led approaches.)

USAID representatives reported that certain features of stakeholders' participation in FTF increased as a result of coordination (see table 7). About half or more of USAID representatives reported that the following three features of stakeholders' participation in FTF increased for all stakeholders: integration of stakeholders' key priorities, formation of partnerships that included the stakeholders, and engagement of stakeholders with other FTF project partners.

**Table 7: Percentage of USAID Representatives Who Reported That Certain Features of Feed the Future (FTF) Planning and Implementation Increased as a Result of Coordination**

| Feature of stakeholders' participation in FTF | Stakeholder type | | | |
|---|---|---|---|---|
| | Host government | Nonprofits | Donors | For-profits |
| Integration of stakeholders' key priorities | 74 | 58 | 64 | 59 |
| Formation of partnerships that included the stakeholders | 68 | 54 | 61 | 57 |
| Engagement of stakeholders with other FTF project partners | 58 | 59 | 50 | 51 |
| Involvement of stakeholders in FTF project implementation | 58 | 53 | 48 | 52 |
| Stakeholders' commitment to FTF project objectives | 55 | 51 | 46 | 53 |
| Stakeholders' capacity to participate in FTF planning or implementation | 54 | 52 | 41 | 50 |

Source: GAO survey.

Notes: All point estimates had a margin of error of no more than plus or minus 4 percentage points. This table presents the features for which the largest percentages of USAID representatives reported that the features increased across all the stakeholder groups. These features were generally reported to have increased by about half or more of the USAID respondents. The features are rank ordered by the reported increases for host government stakeholders. For the full list of features, see Q49, Q56, Q63, and Q70 in the e-supplement (GAO-13-815SP).

## USAID Has Made Some Progress in Monitoring Risks to the Country-Led Approach

Since 2010, USAID has made some progress in monitoring risks related to the country-led approach by developing a tool—the FTF Scorecard—that tracks performance goals on country ownership and includes measures that address risks to the country-led approach. In prior work, we have concluded that agencies may address management challenges and program risks by setting goals and measures related to those challenges and risks.[42] In our May 2008 and March 2010 reports on U.S. global food security efforts, we found deficiencies in measuring and monitoring progress in food security and risks associated with the country-led approach.[43] In our current study, we found that USAID's 2012 and 2013 FTF Scorecards outline two goals to ensure country ownership and sustainability: focus countries lead collaborative implementation of the CIP and local capacity is increasingly able to sustain food security.

---

[42]See GAO, *Managing for Results: Opportunities for Continued Improvements in Agencies' Performance Plans*, GAO-99-215 (Washington, DC: July 20, 1999).This is consistent with the GPRA Modernization Act of 2010, which states that agencies' performance planning should discuss plans to address major management challenges, including through relevant performance goals, indicators, and milestones.

[43]GAO-08-680 and GAO-10-352.

Under these goals, USAID is monitoring five performance measures related to the country-led approach: number of (1) focus countries with increased public expenditure for agriculture; (2) focus countries using outreach platforms to civil society organizations (CSOs) and private sector companies to inform CIP development and implementation; (3) focus countries holding joint sector reviews with donors, CSOs, and private sector firms; (4) focus countries with improved ranking in the World Bank's ease-of-doing-business index;[44] and (5) private enterprises and CSOs that applied new technologies or management practices.[45]

We found that each of these five performance measures on country ownership is related to a risk to the sustainability of U.S. food security investments. Broadly, these measures fall into four risk-related categories: the ability of host governments to meet agriculture funding commitments; stakeholder consultations in the development and implementation of CIPs; host government policies that are conducive to private sector investment; and building local capacity. In our March 2010 report, we found that the country-led approach was vulnerable to a number of risks, including the weak capacity of host governments to meet funding commitments for agriculture and difficulties aligning host government and donor strategies due to differences in policy priorities.[46] Additionally, other FTF guidance documents outlined the necessity of effective consultation with stakeholders, a policy environment conducive for investment, and building local capacity to ensure FTF's sustainability. In fiscal year 2012, of the five country-led measures, results reported in the FTF Scorecard

---

[44]The World Bank *Doing Business* project ranks countries on areas of business regulation. A high ranking on the ease-of-doing-business index means the regulatory environment is more conducive to starting and operating a local firm. See http://www.doingbusiness.org/.

[45]In October 2012, USAID published the FTF Scorecard with fiscal year 2012 targets, as well as cumulative targets for fiscal years 2010-2014. In June 2013, USAID published the FTF Scorecard with fiscal year 2012 targets and actual results achieved.

[46]GAO-10-352. In 2010, we recommended that State delineate measures to mitigate risks associated with the country-led approach. To address some of these risks, State has begun to implement this recommendation by providing support to countries in the development of their food security plans and by reviewing these plans before committing a higher level of U.S. funding.

- *exceeded two targets*: number of focus countries with increased public expenditure for agriculture and private enterprises and number of CSOs that applied new technologies or management practices;
- *partially met two targets*: number of focus countries using outreach platforms to engage civil society and private sector stakeholders in CIP development and implementation and number of focus countries with an improved Doing Business ranking; and
- *did not meet one target*: number of focus countries holding joint sector reviews.[47]

FTF officials who reviewed CIPs in 2010 said the host governments' consultations with their stakeholders were initially weak because host governments had limited time to complete their plans and that in some cases they consulted with stakeholders primarily in capital cities rather than rural areas.

USAID has taken some steps and is planning others to improve stakeholder consultations with host governments and to increase private sector investment in agriculture. The fiscal year 2013 FTF strategic plan states that FTF intends to strengthen the engagement of civil society and private sector stakeholders. According to USAID officials, at least four African focus countries will hold joint sector reviews in 2013. In response to the need to increase the participation of civil society and private sector stakeholders in the CAADP process, USAID sponsored the Africa Lead program to, among other things, build the capacity of civil society and private sector stakeholders to engage more effectively in the implementation of African countries' CIPs.[48] FTF has also sought to increase private sector participation in agriculture, recognizing the importance of these stakeholders to food security efforts. Part of this effort was the creation of the New Alliance for Food Security and Nutrition at the 2012 G8 Summit, in which global and local companies in Africa

---

[47]In fiscal year 2012, the results and targets for each of the five measures were reported as: focus countries with increased public expenditure for agriculture (12 of 10), private enterprises and CSOs that applied new technologies or management practices (44,100 of 26,000), focus countries using outreach platforms to CSOs and private sector companies to inform CIP development and implementation (8 of 10), focus countries with an improved "Doing Business" ranking (6 of 8), and focus countries holding joint sector reviews with donors, CSOs, and private sector firms (0 of 5). The *Doing Business* report ranks countries on 11 areas of business regulation.

[48]Africa Lead is a capacity-building program that provides leadership training, among other things, to public, civil society, and private sector institutions to support the CAADP.

committed more than $3 billion in investments.[49] However, similar programs to improve stakeholder consultations and private sector investment do not exist in the seven Asian and Latin American focus countries.

## USAID Did Not Systematically Assess Risks Related to the Country-Led Approach in Its Multiyear Country Strategies

Although USAID has made some progress at the headquarters level to monitor and address risks to the country-led approach, we found that USAID's FTF multiyear country strategies did not systematically assess these risks.[50] According to USAID's Risk Assessment Guide, a risk assessment informs agency management of the relevant risks associated with achieving management objectives and is intended to help management identify and document risks, prioritize them in terms of susceptibility, and determine the adequacy of controls to manage those risks.[51] A key characteristic of a national strategy is a risk assessment, including an analysis of the threats to, and vulnerabilities of, critical assets and operations.[52] The FTF multiyear strategies outline the 5-year strategic planning for the U.S. government's global hunger and food security

---

[49]The New Alliance builds upon the progress and commitments made at the 2009 L'Aquila summit and includes specific commitments from African leaders to enhance opportunities for private sector investment in their countries, as well as commitments from local and international private sector partners, who have collectively committed more than $3 billion in investments. In September 2012, the New Alliance expanded from the initial countries of Ethiopia, Ghana, and Tanzania to include Burkina Faso, Côte d'Ivoire, and Mozambique. In June 2013, the New Alliance annouced that it was adding three more countries—Nigeria, Malawi, and Benin.

[50]We defined risks to a country-led approach as those related to host governments, stakeholders, and other donors.

[51]This definition is consistent with GAO's risk management framework based on best practices. See GAO, *Homeland Security: Applying Risk Management Principles to Guide Federal Investments*, GAO-07-386T (Washington, D.C.: Feb. 7, 2007). As we stated above, the FTF Scorecard is a monitoring tool that tracks data on some of the risks; however, it is not clear how these risks were prioritized, and the tool does not determine the adequacy of controls to manage risks.

[52]See GAO, *Combating Terrorism: Evaluation of Selected Characteristics in National Strategies Related to Terrorism*, GAO-04-408T (Washington, D.C.: Feb. 3, 2004); and *Influenza Pandemic: Further Efforts Are Needed to Ensure Clearer Federal Leadership Roles and an Effective National Strategy*, GAO-07-781 (Washington, D.C.: Aug. 14, 2007). We identified risk assessments as a key characteristic of a national strategy by reviewing the Homeland Security Act of 2002, as well as other legislation, presidential directives, and GAO and policy research organization publications. See GAO-04-408T for additional details.

initiative at the country-level.[53] According to these strategies, they represent whole-of-government approaches to address food security and were approved by interagency teams. USAID did not require a risk assessment in its guidance on FTF multiyear strategies.

On the basis of our review of the 19 FTF multiyear country strategies, we found that 12 of the 19 did not specifically discuss risks related to a country-led approach. Our review showed that 7 multiyear country strategies contained sections specifically discussing risks, and roughly half of the identified risks related to the country-led approach, including the weak capacity of host governments and host government policies that inhibit private sector investment. The remaining 12 multiyear country strategies did not contain a section specifically discussing risk, but they each identified challenges to the strategies, at least one of which related to the country-led approach. For example, one African country strategy states that organizational and technical capacity remains a major impediment to implementation of its country-owned agriculture development strategy. Local nongovernmental organizations and the private sector are poorly developed, and weak government institutions and insufficient staffing prevent the government from meeting the scale and pace of implementation required by its country investment plan, according to the strategy.

Across the seven multiyear country strategies with sections describing risks, USAID inconsistently identified plans to mitigate the risks identified. We found that fewer than half of the risks identified had corresponding discussions of mitigation strategies. For example, one African country strategy discusses plans to develop capacity and to promote dialogue between the government and private sector to mitigate the risks posed by limited government capacity and intervention in markets. In contrast, another African country strategy described risks to financial and procurement accountability of projects, but the strategy did not identify any mitigation plans to address these risks.

According to the FTF multiyear country strategies, the strategies may be modified as appropriate, but the guidance on updating them indicates that USAID has made an effort to minimize the need to formally amend these

---

[53]According to USAID, these strategies are to align with the CIPs.

strategies due to the comprehensive process used to develop them.[54] Furthermore, USAID's country guidance documents indicate that USAID has plans to integrate FTF multiyear strategies into broader country strategies—Country Development Cooperation Strategies (CDCS).[55] USAID's guidance for developing the CDCS indicates that country teams must assess risks associated with USAID's development objectives and assess the degree to which officials can identify and control critical risks. USAID officials told us that plans for integrating the multiyear strategies into the CDCS will address the lack of risk assessments in the FTF multiyear strategies. However, the guidance documents for developing the CDCS indicate that country teams have the flexibility to determine the level of integration of their FTF multiyear strategy; moreover, the guidance indicates that some country teams are exempt from the requirement to integrate FTF into their CDCS. The CDCS Supplemental Guidance for Integrating Feed the Future states that USAID country teams receiving FTF funding should demonstrate that they strongly considered integrating FTF planning into the CDCS, but they are not required to do so. Furthermore, the guidance states that the integration of FTF multiyear strategies is not applicable to those USAID country teams that have completed a CDCS or are far along in the CDCS process. Because the integration of FTF multiyear strategies into the CDCS remains an option, and not a requirement, for country teams, the extent to which USAID plans to systematically assess and mitigate risks to the country-led approach remains unclear. Without requirements for FTF country staff to identify and mitigate risks associated with the country-led approach, the U.S. government's ability to achieve its goals for improving global food security could be limited.

## Conclusions

In 2010, President Obama outlined a new operational model for enhancing interagency cooperation and responding to country priorities with broad consultation in global food security programs. This marked a shift from prior policy and efforts, and results from our survey of 19 FTF focus countries strongly suggest that the U.S. government has made good progress in applying a whole-of-government and country-led

---

[54]The FTF multiyear strategy change guidance indicates that possible strategy changes may be deemed necessary due to budgetary, programmatic, interagency policy, host-country, or other considerations.

[55]The CDCS are 5-year development strategies that include discussions of how USAID assistance will be synchronized with other agencies' efforts.

approach. Progress achieved in U.S. interagency coordination and engagement with country stakeholders can enhance U.S. efforts in FTF countries to improve agriculture productivity and reduce malnutrition among children. In addition, by aligning and coordinating its food security efforts with those outlined in each country's investment plan, including efforts of other donors, the U.S. government can ensure a more effective contribution toward the United Nations Millennium Development Goal of eradicating extreme poverty and hunger. However, USAID has not systematically assessed risks to aligning U.S. investments to country priorities and engaging multiple stakeholders. USAID's guidance indicates that risk assessments inform management of the relevant risks associated with achieving objectives and help them determine the adequacy of controls to manage those risks. Although USAID guidance documents indicate that country teams must assess risks associated with USAID's development objectives, the agency does not require FTF country teams to systematically assess and mitigate risks to the FTF's country-led approach.

In the absence of requirements for FTF country staff to identify and mitigate risks in aligning resources with country priorities and engaging multiple stakeholders, further progress in implementing the country-led approach could be hampered and could limit the U.S. government's ability to achieve its goals for improving global food security.

## Recommendations for Executive Action

To ensure that risks related to the country-led approach are systematically assessed, we recommend that the USAID Administrator take the following two actions:

- require FTF country staff to conduct periodic risk assessments associated with pursuing a country-led approach and

- require FTF country staff to develop plans to mitigate any risks identified as part of its periodic risk assessments.

## Agency Comments

We provided a draft of this report for comment to USAID, State, MCC, Treasury, USDA, the Peace Corps, USADF, OMB, and OPIC. USAID provided written comments on a draft of our report. We have reprinted these comments in appendix VI. USAID concurred with both of our recommendations and outlined steps to revise their guidance to be more explicit about risk assessments and mitigation strategies for the country-led approach. We also received technical comments from USAID, USDA, State, and USADF, which we have incorporated, as appropriate.

We are sending a copy of this report to interested congressional committees and to the Administrator of USAID; the Secretaries of State, Treasury, and Agriculture; the Directors of the OMB and the Peace Corps; and the Chief Executive Officers of MCC, OPIC, and USADF. In addition, the report will be available at no charge on the GAO website at http://www.gao.gov.

If you or your staff have any questions regarding this report, please contact me at (202) 512-9601 or MelitoT@gao.gov. Contact points for our Offices of Congressional Relations and Public Affairs may be found on the last page of this report. GAO staff who made key contributions to this report are listed in appendix VII.

Thomas Melito
Director, International Affairs and Trade

# Appendix I: Objectives, Scope, and Methodology

This report is part of a larger of body of work we have undertaken reviewing the U.S. government's efforts to improve international food security, including reports we issued in 2008 and 2010.[56] This report specifically examines (1) the extent to which the U.S. Agency for International Development (USAID) has applied a whole-of-government approach and (2) how USAID has facilitated a country-led approach for the Feed the Future (FTF) initiative. This report is primarily based on our survey of U.S FTF agency representatives in the 19 FTF focus countries and on our review of FTF documents.

To determine the extent to which USAID has applied a whole-of-government approach and to assess how USAID has facilitated a country-led approach, we collected and reviewed agency documents. We also assessed whether coordination was consistent with key practices that enhance and sustain interagency collaboration and key features that benefit interagency collaboration mechanisms identified in prior GAO reports.[57] To identify how USAID outlined these two approaches, we reviewed agency FTF planning documents including FTF implementation plans, strategic reviews and multiyear strategies, and other agency specific food security planning documents such as the U.S. Department of Agriculture's 2011 and 2012 food security plans. We also reviewed FTF guidance documents such as the 2010 Feed the Future Guide, 2010 Quadrennial Diplomacy and Development Review, focus country strategic reviews, the 2010 Feed the Future Multiyear Strategy Guidance, Feed the Future Indicator Handbook, and FTF-related agency cables. Furthermore, we reviewed the 2012 and 2013 Feed the Future Progress Report and

---

[56]See GAO, *International Food Security: Insufficient Efforts by Host Governments and Donors Threaten Progress to Halve Hunger in Sub-Saharan Africa by 2015*, GAO-08-680 (Washington, D.C.: May 29, 2008), and *Global Food Security: U.S. Agencies Progressing on Governmentwide Strategy, but Approach Faces Several Vulnerabilities*, GAO-10-352 (Washington, D.C.: Mar. 11, 2010).

[57]GAO, *Results-Oriented Government: Practices That Can Help Enhance and Sustain Collaboration among Federal Agencies*, GAO-06-15 (Washington, D.C.: Oct. 21, 2005) and *Key Considerations for Implementing Interagency Collaborative Mechanisms*, GAO-12-1022 (Washington, D.C.: Sept. 27, 2012). To identify key practices, we reviewed academic literature and prior GAO and Congressional Research Service reports. In addition, we interviewed experts in coordination, collaboration, partnerships, and networks such as the National Academy of Public Administration. See GAO-06-15 and GAO-12-1022 for additional details.

Feed the Future Scorecard for the most recent program monitoring
information available.[58]

To determine the extent to which USAID and FTF partner agency
representatives believe that they were implementing a whole-of-
government approach and country-led approach in planning and
implementing FTF, we conducted interviews with officials in Washington,
D.C., from USAID, Department of State (State), Millennium Challenge
Corporation (MCC), Department of the Treasury (Treasury), Department
of Agriculture (USDA), the Peace Corps, U.S. African Development
Foundation (USADF), Overseas Private Investment Corporation (OPIC),
and the Office of Management and Budget. To obtain the views of
USAID's and FTF partner agencies' in-country representatives on these
topics, we sent a web-based survey to all representatives identified by
their agency as key FTF personnel for the 19 FTF countries. The survey
asked their perceptions of the whole-of-government and country-led
approaches in the planning and implementation of FTF. The topics
included coordination within and between U.S. agencies, coordination
with country stakeholders, the mechanism and frequency of coordination,
the perceived effectiveness of the coordination, and factors that may have
helped or hindered coordination. The questionnaire and survey results
are available in an e-supplement (GAO-13-815SP).

To identify key personnel for each country, we asked USAID to provide a
list of all key personnel for each country, including personnel from other
agencies. We verified the non-USAID key personnel with each relevant
agency. Since each FTF focus country is different in terms of the
agencies involved, the FTF programs and activities, and the levels of
commitment from the various embassy and in-country staff, there is no
consistent definition of what constitutes a "key" person involved in FTF;
for that reason, the population was defined for us by the FTF agencies.
Key personnel included mission directors, Foreign Service Officers,
Foreign Service Nationals, and personal services contractors. The final
list of key personnel included 551 individuals, the majority of whom were
USAID employees (see table 8). We did not survey focus-country
stakeholders, such as country government representatives, about the

---

[58]We presented 2012 performance data as reported by USAID for contextual purposes,
and did not independently verify the data.

U.S. government country-led approach in the planning and
implementation of FTF.

**Table 8: Feed the Future (FTF) Survey Response Rates, by Agency**

|  | Total number identified as key personnel | Total number determined to be out of scope | Total number of responses | Response rate (percentage)[a] |
|---|---|---|---|---|
| USAID | 376 | 28 | 252 | 74 |
| FTF partners | 175 | 24 | 90 | 65 |
| State | 91 | 13 | 36 | 54 |
| USDA | 18 | 3 | 15 | 100 |
| Peace Corps | 21 | 1 | 17 | 86 |
| Other partners | 45 | 7 | 22 | 64 |
| **Total** | **551** | **52** | **342** | **72** |

Legend: USAID = U.S. Agency for International Development; State = Department of State; USDA = U.S. Department of Agriculture.

Source. GAO survey.

Notes: After sending out the survey, we identified 52 key personnel who had left their post prior to our sending out the survey request, who told us that they did not work on FTF, who were U.S.-based, or who were otherwise out of scope.

[a]We used Response Rate 3 (RR3) as defined by the American Association for Public Opinion Research in *Standard Definitions: Final Dispositions of Case Codes and Outcome Rates for Surveys*, 7th ed., 2011. Weighting accounts for the unequal agency sizes and response rates across agencies.

We sent the web-based survey to all 551 key personnel on May 21, 2012 and administered the survey until August 31, 2012. To increase response rates, we sent several follow-up e-mails to agency officials and made telephone calls to nonrespondents. After sending out the survey, we identified 52 key personnel who had left their post prior to our sending out the survey request, who told us that they did not work on FTF, who were U.S.-based, or who were otherwise out of scope. This reduced our list of key personnel to 499. Overall, we achieved a weighted response rate of 72 percent, with 342 respondents to our survey.[59] Agency response rates are shown in table 8.

---

[59]We used Response Rate 3 (RR3) as defined by the American Association for Public Opinion Research in *Standard Definitions: Final Dispositions of Case Codes and Outcome Rates for Surveys*, 7th ed., 2011. Weighting accounts for the unequal agency sizes and response rates across agencies.

Using information available to us for all survey recipients, such as
employment status, we conducted a nonresponse bias analysis.[60] The
nonresponse bias analysis did not find any statistically measurable bias
that would affect our analyses. Therefore, although our survey was
intended to be a census, for the purposes of analyzing the results, we
decided to treat our survey as a random sample. Unless otherwise noted,
point estimates we report for 2012 have a margin of error of no more than
plus or minus 9 percentage points at the 95 percent level of confidence.

The practical difficulties of conducting any survey may also introduce
nonsampling errors, such as difficulties interpreting a particular question,
which can introduce unwanted variability into the survey results. We took
steps to minimize nonsampling errors by pretesting the questionnaire
over the telephone with six in-country officials from USAID or FTF partner
agencies in March and April 2012, including three from USAID (one of
whom was a Foreign Service National) and one each from State, USDA,
and the Peace Corps. We conducted pretests to make sure that the
questions were clear and unbiased and that the questionnaire did not
place an undue burden on respondents. An independent reviewer within
GAO also reviewed a draft of the questionnaire prior to its administration.
We made appropriate revisions to the content and format of the
questionnaire after the pretests and independent review.

To determine the extent to which USAID has identified risks and
documented efforts to mitigate them in the FTF multiyear strategies, we
completed the following analyses. We focused on risk assessments
because in reports issued in 2004 and 2007 we identified a risk
assessment as one of several key characteristics of a national strategy.
Additionally, a risk assessment should include an analysis of the threats
to, and vulnerabilities of, critical assets and operations.[61] First, we

---

[60]A nonresponse bias analysis is used to verify that nonrespondents to the survey would
not answer differently from those who did respond and that the respondents are
representative of the target population, thus ensuring that the results can be generalized
to the population from which the sample was chosen.

[61]See GAO, *Combating Terrorism: Evaluation of Selected Characteristics in National
Strategies Related to Terrorism*, GAO-04-408T (Washington, D.C.: Feb. 3, 2004);
*Influenza Pandemic: Further Efforts Are Needed to Ensure Clearer Federal Leadership
Roles and an Effective National Strategy*, GAO-07-781 (Washington, D.C.: Aug. 14,
2007). Risk assessment as a key characteristic of a national strategy was identified by
reviewing the Homeland Security Act of 2002, as well as other legislation, presidential
directives, and GAO and policy research organization publications.

reviewed and analyzed the multiyear strategies for all 19 FTF countries to identify those strategies that had a section dedicated to listing and describing "risks" to the FTF program. We found that 7 of the 19 strategies had specific risk sections. Second, we conducted an analysis on the types of risks found in the 7 strategies with specific risk sections. We found that a total of 44 risks were listed in these strategies and coded them according to whether they pertained to the key stakeholders in country (host governments, in-country for-profit sector, in-country nonprofit sector, and other donors) or whether they pertained to other, broader risks, such as natural resources or market conditions. We did this to determine the number of risks that pertain to key stakeholders because FTF considers these groups essential to implementing the country-led approach. Of the 44 risks, 25 pertained to key stakeholders and 19 pertained to other, broader risks. For each of the 44 risks, we looked for a mitigation strategy that was directly tied to the listed risk. We recognize that, in some instances, other sections of the report described steps that U.S. agencies could take to address the risks to some degree. However, our purpose was not to assess the actions the U.S. government was taking to address risks, but to determine whether it was following a systematic risk assessment process. We found that 21 of the 44 risks had mitigation strategies and 23 did not. Third, for the 12 strategies without specific risk sections, we reviewed other sections in the reports listing and examining concepts related to risk, such as "challenges," "barriers," "limitations," or "concerns." We also reviewed the strategies to determine whether they included a section referred to as "Development Challenges and Opportunities," as required by USAID's FTF multiyear strategy guidance. In addition, we determined whether each strategy included any challenges related to key stakeholders (host governments, in-country for-profit sector, in-country nonprofit sector, and other donors), who are central to FTF's country-led approach. We found an example of these key stakeholder issues in each of the 12 strategies. To perform these analyses, two analysts independently reviewed all 19 multiyear strategies, identified the risks or related issues, and coded the risks or issues according to whether they pertained to key stakeholders. The analysts worked iteratively, comparing notes and reconciling differences at each stage of the analysis. In addition, the final analysis was reviewed by other GAO staff independent of the two analysts, and modifications were made as appropriate.

To identify the amount of funding provided to FTF, we obtained and analyzed allocations and disbursement data for FTF and FTF-related programs such as USAID Title II Food for Peace and USDA McGovern-Dole Food for Education for fiscal years 2010 through 2013 as of March

31, 2013, for each agency. The information reported as allocations and disbursements was provided to us by the agencies. We use the term "allocations" to refer to funds the agencies reported that they directed to FTF. We did not independently assess the amounts agencies reported as allocations and disbursements. We also did not assess the extent to which the funds directed to FTF have been obligated. The agencies reported some differences in the ways that they provided data on allocations and disbursements for FTF, which we list as notes in table 2. We interviewed the agencies about the data and determined they were sufficient for background purposes in our report.

We conducted this performance audit from March 2013 to September 2013 in accordance with generally accepted government auditing standards. Those standards require that we plan and perform the audit to obtain sufficient, appropriate evidence to provide a reasonable basis for our findings and conclusions based on our audit objectives. We believe that the evidence obtained provides a reasonable basis for our findings and conclusions based on our audit objectives.

# Appendix II: Other U.S. Global Food Security Programs Related to Feed the Future

The Feed the Future (FTF) initiative incorporates other U.S. assistance programs related to global food security that are implemented by the U.S. Agency for International Development, the Department of the Treasury, and the U.S. Department of Agriculture (USDA). Each of these other programs addresses global food security and other development challenges, as described in table 9.

**Table 9: Other U.S. Global Food Security Programs Related to the Feed the Future (FTF) Initiative**

| FTF-related program | Description |
|---|---|
| U.S. Agency for International Development | |
| Food for Peace Title II Development Food Assistance | The Title II development assistance includes the donation of commodities to meet nonemergency needs as well as the sale of commodities in-country to obtain funds for development purposes, including food security goals. |
| Nutrition (Global Health Programs) | These programs provide technical leadership and direction in nutrition and food security with a focus on infant and young child nutrition, micronutrient supplementation, food fortification, and developing innovative products to improve diet quality for sustainable nutrition. |
| Millennium Challenge Corporation | |
| Food Security Investments | These programs include the development of irrigation systems in Burkina Faso, livestock and land and water resource management in Mongolia, fruit tree and fisheries sector development in Morocco, Coconut sector development in Mozambique, rangeland and livestock management and indigenous natural product sector development in Namibia, and feed and market roads rehabilitation and construction in Tanzania. |
| Department of the Treasury | |
| International Fund for Agricultural Development | Through this specialized agency of the United Nations, the Department of the Treasury, along with other international donors, invests in agricultural development, including rural development and policy reform. |
| U.S. Department of Agriculture (USDA) | |
| McGovern-Dole Food for Education | This program donates U.S. agricultural commodities and financial and technical assistance for school feeding and maternal and child nutrition projects in low-income, food-insecure countries committed to universal education. |
| Food for Progress | This program provides for the donation or credit sale of U.S. commodities to developing countries and emerging democracies committed to introducing and expanding free enterprise in the agricultural sector. In most cases, commodities are sold in-country to support agricultural projects to increase rural incomes and enhance food security. |
| Local and Regional Procurement Pilot Project | This pilot program purchased local and regional food products to help meet nonemergency food needs in developing countries during fiscal years 2008 through 2012. One program objective was to provide a basis for determining the efficacy and impact of local and regional procurement of food aid. |
| Food Aid Nutrition Enhancement Competitive Grants | This program provides grants for improving the nutritional content, product composition, packaging, and other components of food products delivered through humanitarian assistance program to enhance the short- and long-term health of individuals, especially infants and young children. |
| Cochran Fellowship | This program provides participants from middle-income countries, emerging markets, and emerging democracies with high-quality training to improve their local agricultural systems and strengthen and enhance trade links. |

| FTF-related program | Description |
|---|---|
| Norman E. Borlaug International Agricultural Science and Technology Fellowship | This program promotes food security and economic growth by providing research and training opportunities for scientists and policymakers from developing and middle-income countries. USDA partners with U.S. land grant universities, international research centers, and other institutions to provide up to 12 weeks of U.S.-based training for Borlaug Fellows each year. |

Source: GAO analysis of agency documents.

# Appendix III: Illustrative Example of USAID Representatives' Reported Coordination with Feed the Future Partner Agencies in One Country

Figure 3 presents an illustrative example of U.S. Agency for International Development (USAID) representatives' reported coordination with Feed the Future (FTF) partner agencies in one country. We selected this country because (1) the number of USAID staff working on FTF represented the average for the 19 countries and (2) the country had a very high response rate to the survey. In this example, the USAID staff members are organized by the Mission Director and Deputy Director, Foreign Service Officers, Personal Services Contractors, and Foreign Service Nationals. For the diagram, we used generic rather than specific job titles for the USAID staff to ensure confidentiality. In addition, to simplify the example, we combined information we received from several survey respondents who reported similar or miscellaneous titles.

**Figure 3: Illustrative Example of USAID's Reported Coordination with Feed the Future (FTF) Partner Agencies in One Mission**

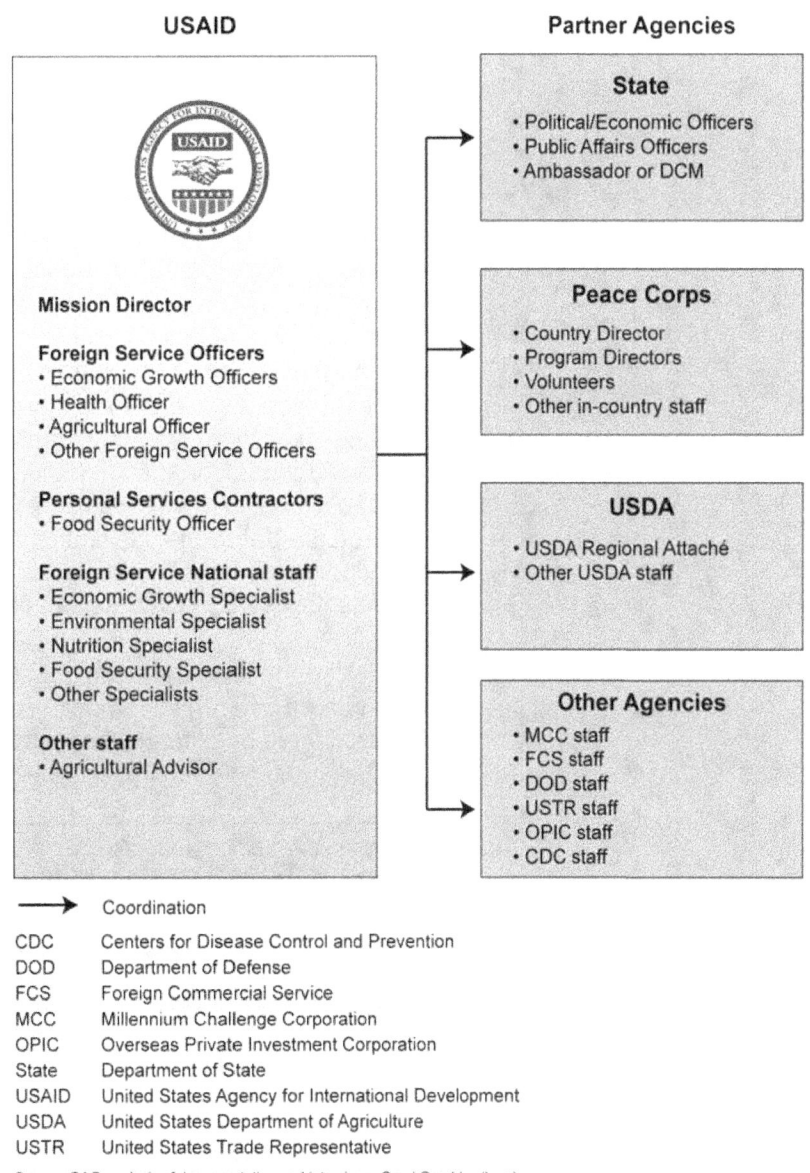

| | Coordination |
|---|---|
| CDC | Centers for Disease Control and Prevention |
| DOD | Department of Defense |
| FCS | Foreign Commercial Service |
| MCC | Millennium Challenge Corporation |
| OPIC | Overseas Private Investment Corporation |
| State | Department of State |
| USAID | United States Agency for International Development |
| USDA | United States Department of Agriculture |
| USTR | United States Trade Representative |

Source: GAO analysis of documentation and interviews; Corel Graphics (logo).

Notes: USAID staff reporting similar positions were combined in this chart. Staff reporting miscellaneous positions were listed as "Other staff." Regional USAID staff were not included in this chart. The "Partner Agencies" are ordered by the number of USAID staff that reported coordinating with them. The named staff positions within each partner agency are ordered by the number of USAID staff that reported coordinating with them, except for "Other staff," who are always placed at the bottom of every category.

# Appendix IV: Multiple Regression Analysis of Survey Results to Identify Predictors of Perceived Effectiveness of Coordination

In analyzing the results of our survey of several hundred U.S. representatives with duties related to the Feed the Future (FTF) initiative in 19 focus countries, we explored whether certain factors could help explain differences in how U.S. representatives perceived coordination related to FTF. To what extent were such factors as the U.S. representatives' different agencies, roles, and positions predictive of differences in their perceptions of FTF coordination? To answer that question, we used data from a series of questions in which the U.S. representatives assessed the effectiveness of their coordination in accomplishing eight specific actions, such as developing or contributing to integrated FTF program documents.[62] Depending on how many agencies the representatives reported coordinating with, the questions were presented up to five times to obtain perceptions of the effectiveness of their coordination with representatives in their own and other agencies.[63] We constructed a scale from responses to all coordination effectiveness questions, allocating each representative a point for each action for which they viewed their coordination as "very effective" or "somewhat effective." Thus, the maximum score was 40 points for representatives who answered the questions five times and each time rated their coordination as very or somewhat effective for all eight actions; on average each respondent rated 8.5 activities as very or somewhat effective.[64]

In analyzing the raw scores on the coordination effectiveness scale, we found marked differences among representatives when we grouped and compared them by different tenures in their jobs, different agencies, and

---

[62]The other seven actions were integrating FTF program or project planning with other U.S. foreign assistance programs; sharing observations or information obtained through meetings with host government officials; sharing observations or information obtained through meetings with other stakeholders; making progress on needed policy reforms in host country; identifying donors and partners; developing joint or compatible procedures or processes for FTF activities (e.g., action plans, donor coordination procedures, etc); and developing joint communication plans, reports and/or cables. Additionally, the survey asked about "other actions" that were affected by coordination, but these were not included in our measure.

[63]Representatives were presented with the same series of questions about effectiveness of coordination for each of four agencies—the USAID, State, USDA, and the Peace Corps. The series of questions was also presented to elicit responses regarding coordination with FTF staff from all other agencies at the representative's post.

[64]To test the reliability of the scale, we examined Cronbach's alpha, a measure of whether the variation in the scale captures the majority of the variation in the underlying items. Our scale had a Cronbach's alpha of .95, which meets professionally accepted standards for the reliability of a scale.

different amounts of time on FTF activities. For example, representatives who reported spending very little of their time on FTF activities viewed their coordination as effective in accomplishing an average of 4 actions, compared with an average of 9 for representatives who reported spending most of their time on FTF activities. Similarly, Department of State (State) representatives on average viewed their coordination as effective for about 12 actions, compared with an average of 8 for nonregional representatives of the lead FTF agency, the U.S. Agency for International Development (USAID).

We used regression analysis to assess whether such differences in perceptions of effectiveness across representatives as measured by our scale persisted after controlling for other factors, such as different roles, positions, and opportunities to engage in the actions specified in the coordination effectiveness questions. Regression analysis allowed us to assess the unique association between our outcome variable and a given predictor variable,[65] while controlling for multiple other predictor variables. In our ordinary least squares (OLS) regression model, we controlled for a variety of demographic factors that might have an impact on perceptions of effectiveness, including representatives' agency (USAID, State, the U.S. Department of Agriculture, the Peace Corps, and all other partner agencies); their tenure (less than a year, a year to less than 2 years, and 2 years or more); their employment status (Foreign Service Officers/Foreign Service Officers Limited, Foreign Service Nationals, and all others including contractors); the amount of time spent on FTF activities (very little, some or about half, and most or all); the number of entities the representative reported coordinating with; and, for USAID representatives, whether the representative was considered a regional representative. Additionally, we also examined whether the representative reported coordinating with USAID (or other USAID representatives) and how many USAID staff they coordinated with. Finally, we used information from previous GAO research to identify certain factors that potentially affect coordination. For example, we included indicators for whether representatives felt that specific factors helped or hindered

---

[65]The outcome variable is also referred to as the dependent variable, and predictor variables are also referred to as independent variables.

coordination overall, including funding, staffing levels, clarity of roles and responsibilities, and the compatibility of performance measures.[66]

Our regression model identified several factors that had statistically significant associations with representatives' perceptions of the effectiveness of their coordination, after controlling for other factors.[67] Notably, State representatives, representatives with intermediate job tenure, and representatives who reported spending some to half their time on FTF activities had mean scores on the coordination effectiveness scale that were significantly higher than, respectively, USAID representatives, representatives with less job tenure, and representatives who spent less time on FTF. Additionally, we found that on average, representatives who felt, respectively, that staffing levels at their agencies, clarity of roles and responsibilities, and compatibility of performance measures and representatives helped with coordination also had significantly higher mean scores on the coordination effectiveness scale than those who felt these factors had no effect or had no opinion on them. After controlling for other factors, we did not find a significant association between representatives' perceptions of coordination effectiveness and their employment status (Foreign Service Officer/Foreign Service Officer Limited, Foreign Service National or Locally Employed Staff, and Personal Services Contractor/Others) regional status (for USAID representatives), or views on whether the amount of funding helped or hindered coordination activities. Table 10 presents the categorical predictor variables in the regression model

---

[66]These indicators were derived from the Q32 question series, which asks representatives to rate field-based coordination among all US government representatives, and specifically whether certain factors such as communication, funding or staffing have helped or hindered coordination.

[67]The associations are identified by regression coefficients, which are considered to be statistically significant at the $p \leq .05$ level. This indicates that there is a 5 percent or lower chance that a coefficient would be as large as it is if there were no relationship between the variable and the outcome variable. Because it is possible that the failure to identify significant coefficients is partly a function of the relatively small sample size (327 observations with full data in the regression), we also examined several variables that were consistently significant across models at the $p \leq .10$ level, and note that these variables are not significant at traditional levels.

variables for which statistically significant associations were found with
the outcome variable.[68]

**Table 10: Categorical Variables in the Regression Model for Which at Least One Respondent Group Had a Significantly Higher Mean Number of Actions for Which Coordination Was Effective**

| Factor | Respondent group for which regression coefficient was statistically significant[a] | Reference respondent group for comparison | Other respondent groups for which regression coefficient was not statistically significant |
|---|---|---|---|
| Agency | State | USAID nonregional | USAID regional, USDA, and all other agencies |
| Tenure | More than 1 year to 2 years | 1 year or less | More than 2 years |
| Time spent on Feed the Future (FTF) activities | Combined: Some of my time / About half of my time | Very little of my time | Most of my time / All of my time[b] |
| Clarity on roles and responsibilities | Clarity helped | No effect / No opinion | Clarity hindered |
| Staffing levels in the field at own agency | Staffing levels helped | No effect / No opinion | Staffing levels hindered |
| Compatibility of performance goals and measures | Compatibility helped | No effect / No opinion | Compatibility hindered |

Legend: State = Department of State; USAID = U.S. Agency for International Development; USDA = U.S. Department of Agriculture.

Source: GAO survey.

Notes:

[a]Coefficients for these response groups were considered to be statistically significant at the $p \leq .05$ level. This indicates that there is a 5 percent or lower chance that a coefficient would be as large as it is if there were no relationship between the variable and the outcome variable.

[b]This variable was positively associated with the number of activities seen as effective at the $p \leq .10$ level.

In developing our final model, we tested multiple versions of our model to evaluate the functional form of the relationships it specified and to ensure that the results were robust across specifications. We included core demographic variables in all models under consideration, including tenure, time spent on FTF, employment status, agency, and the number of entities the representative reported coordinating with. We tested additional predictor variables that surfaced as potentially important through our research, but decided against including in our final model all

[68]The one continuous predictor variable in the model also showed a statistically significant association with the outcome variable: the number of USAID representatives that each survey respondent reported coordinating with.

non-significant variables tested because of the limited number of representatives responding to our survey.[69] Conversely, in some cases, we included in our final model several variables that were important controls or theoretically important but did not rise to the level of statistical significance. Most notably, because our outcome variable is constrained by the number of the five different agencies that each representative reported working with, all models included a control for this factor.[70]

We conducted a variety of other tests to check for high leverage outliers, model fit, and other issues. We did not find evidence of consistently high leverage points or outliers that appeared to have undue influence on our coefficients or model variance. We also checked across a variety of specifications, including different variables and functional forms, to ensure that the final model results were fairly stable across specifications in terms of the substantive and statistical significance of the coefficients (in terms of direction, magnitude, and significance). For example, because our outcome variable is highly skewed, we tested our model using different functional forms (including a logged outcome variable and a Poisson count model) to ensure that the interpretation of the results was consistent with our final model using OLS. We decided to use an OLS specification despite the skew in the outcome variable for several reasons, including the consistency of interpretation with the alternative models tested, the relative robustness of OLS to violations of functional forms, and the ease of interpreting the regression coefficients. Our final model had an R2 of 0.398, suggesting that the predictor variables predicted approximately 40 percent of the variation in the outcome variable.

[69]This included, for example, additional questions from the q32 question series. We checked for stability of coefficients and degradation of fit by comparing model $R^2$ statistics before and after to drop variables that were not statistically significant.

[70]Our final model treats the variable as categorical, to allow for different effects at different levels of coordination with other agencies. No individual category in our model was statistically significant compared with those who did not report coordinating with any other entities. Results from the final model were also generally consistent with a version of the model that included a categorical variable of the number of activities (out of the 40 possible in the dependent variable) for which each respondent reported a positive or negative opinion.

# Appendix V: Feed the Future Partner Agencies' Approaches to Country-Led Program Implementation

The country-led approaches to implementing food security programs by Feed the Future (FTF) partner agencies vary according to particular agency mandates and agency roles in FTF. The following examples illustrate the variation in approaches by the Millennium Challenge Corporation (MCC), the Peace Corps, the U.S. Department of State (State), the U.S. Department of the Treasury (Treasury), the U.S. African Development Foundation (USADF), and the U.S. Department of Agriculture (USDA).

- **MCC**: MCC has been using the country ownership approach to development since its inception in 2004. MCC provides assistance to eligible countries through multiyear compact agreements including agriculture-related investments. Partner country governments are responsible for the implementation of MCC compacts, including initiating a meaningful consultative process with the country's civil society, nongovernmental organization, and private sector stakeholders, as well as a broad range of government stakeholders.
- **Peace Corps**: Peace Corps officials described their approach to country ownership as working with partner countries from the national level down to the community level and engaging their volunteers in projects that are supported by host country governments. In addition, each project has a Project Advisory Committee that contributes to the design and evaluation of the project and includes at least one representative from the government and local community.
- **State**: State was the lead agency for Feed the Future from 2009 to 2010 and led the development of the FTF Guide, which described the FTF country-led approach. State officials have promoted stakeholder consultations around the development of country investment plans and have also helped facilitate greater civil society and private sector involvement in FTF.
- **Treasury**: Treasury officials work with the World Bank's multidonor trust fund Global Agriculture and Food Security Program (GAFSP) and have made efforts to align GAFSP and FTF's country-led approaches. Treasury assisted in the development of the selection criteria for GAFSP funding which includes an assessment of the country's policy environment as well as evidence of consultations with local stakeholders.
- **USADF**: USADF provides grants of up to $250,000 to the most vulnerable communities in Africa and these grants fund projects that are led by staff of local technical partners that engage community groups in the project's design and implementation.
- **USDA**: USDA seeks to align its resources with country investment plans where it concentrates its food security investments. USDA particularly focuses on ensuring that the private sector is included in

food security consultations and works directly with host government
officials and local universities and civil society.

# Appendix VI: Comments from the U.S. Agency for International Development

GAO received USAID letter on September 5, 2013.

Thomas Melito
Director, International Affairs & Trade
U.S. Government Accountability Office
Washington, DC 20548

Dear Mr. Melito:

I am pleased to provide USAID's formal response to the Government Accountability Office (GAO) draft report entitled "Global Food Security: USAID Is Improving Coordination but Needs to Require Systematic Assessments of Country-Level Risks" (GAO-13-809).

This letter, together with the enclosed USAID comments, are provided for incorporation as an appendix to the final report.

Thank you for the opportunity to respond to the GAO draft report and for the courtesies extended by your staff in the conduct of this audit review.

Sincerely,

Angelique M. Crumbly
Assistant Administrator
Bureau for Management
U.S. Agency for International Development

Enclosure: a/s

- 2 -

USAID COMMENTS ON GAO DRAFT REPORT No. GAO-13-809

As the lead implementing agency within the U.S. Government in the area of food security, the U.S. Agency for International Development (USAID) is pleased to offer its comments on the GAO Report to congressional requestors, Global Food Security: USAID Is Improving Coordination but Needs to Require Systematic Assessment of Country-Level Risks. The report comes at an important time as many Feed the Future (FTF) multi-year strategies (MYS) will expire in 2014 and we are looking to more fully integrate them into the Country Development Cooperation Strategies (CDCS).

We are pleased to see GAO acknowledge the very significant progress on whole-of-government coordination and the marked progress on mitigating the risks to the country-led approach. None of this progress could have been achieved without the strong leadership and commitment of all of the agencies/departments guiding the FTF initiative.

**Recommendation 1:** We recommend that USAID require FTF country staff to conduct periodic risk assessments associated with pursuing a country-led approach.

USAID concurs with this recommendation. USAID's commitment to assessing and mitigating risks associated with development programs is reflected in its Automated Directives System (ADS) policy guidance. ADS 201.3.3.3, which establishes policy for the development of the CDCS, provides:

> **Local Capacity Development:** A key strategic consideration is local capacity development. This includes both the use of partner country government systems and the constellation of local organizations in the country and their relationships with government, donors, one another, and the general population. An analysis of local public and private organizations (government, civil society and private sector entities), and how the Mission plans to support the capacity development of these entities should inform the CDCS.
>
> As part of this analysis, the Mission should conduct the Public Financial Management Risk Assessment Framework (PFMRAF) Stage 1 analysis. Capacity development and the qualities of USAID partnership with local entities should be considered at all stages of the Program Cycle.

FTF MYS are subject to comply with the ADS policy in the above paragraph. As we move toward fuller integration of FTF MYS into the CDCS, we will revise the "CDCS Supplemental Guidance for Integrating Feed the Future" to be more explicit about risk assessment and mitigation of the country-led approach. The amended guidance will include the following requirements:

1. All FTF MYS to be fully integrated into CDCS when the next CDCS is developed.

2. If the FTF MYS expires before the next CDCS is developed, then the post must seek, in writing, an extension of the MYS. The justification for extension must include a risk

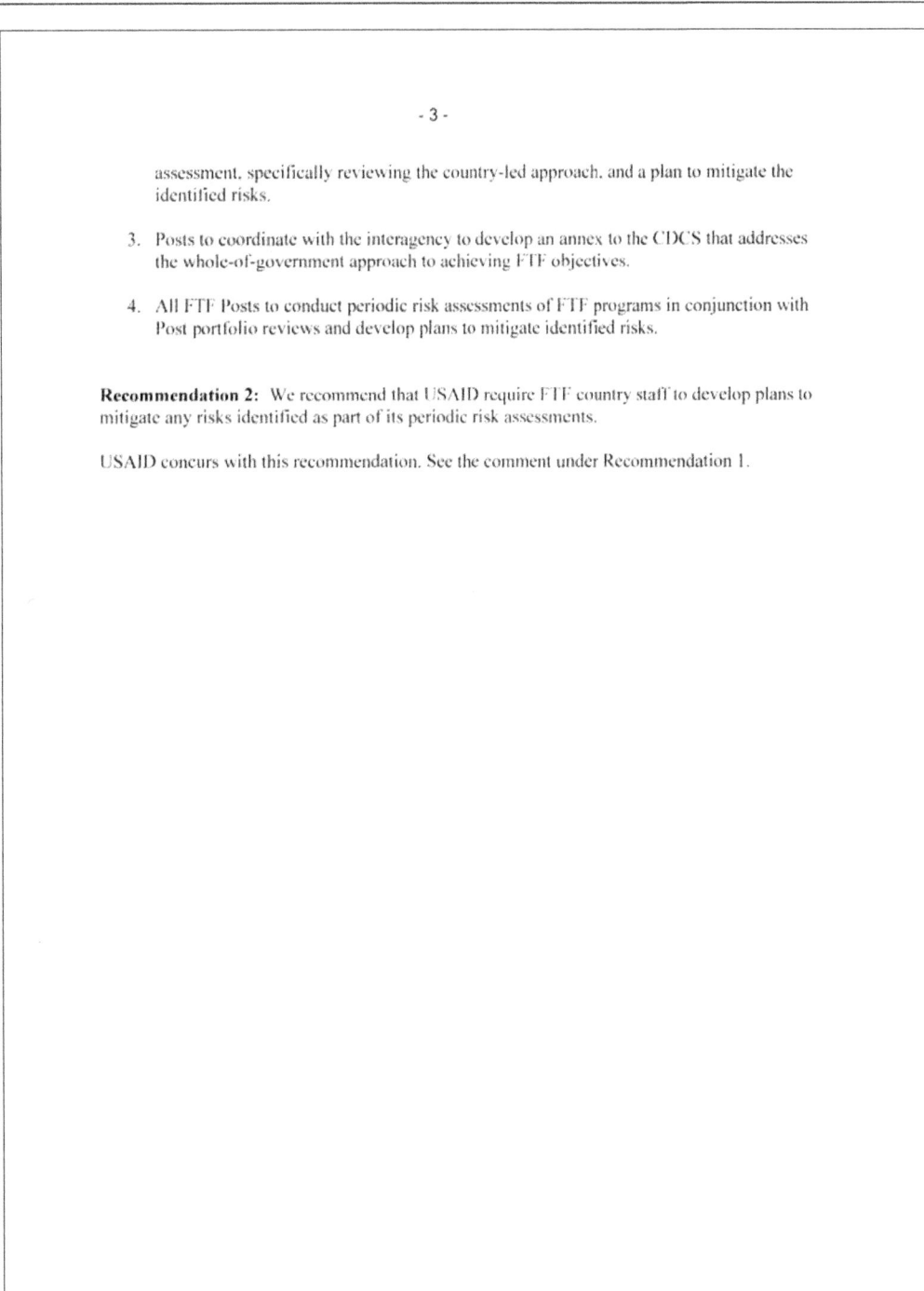

- 3 -

assessment, specifically reviewing the country-led approach, and a plan to mitigate the identified risks.

3.  Posts to coordinate with the interagency to develop an annex to the CDCS that addresses the whole-of-government approach to achieving FTF objectives.

4.  All FTF Posts to conduct periodic risk assessments of FTF programs in conjunction with Post portfolio reviews and develop plans to mitigate identified risks.

**Recommendation 2:** We recommend that USAID require FTF country staff to develop plans to mitigate any risks identified as part of its periodic risk assessments.

USAID concurs with this recommendation. See the comment under Recommendation 1.

# Appendix VII: GAO Contact and Staff Acknowledgments

| | |
|---|---|
| **GAO Contact** | Thomas Melito, (202) 512-9601 or melitot@gao.gov |
| **Staff Acknowledgments** | In addition to the contact named above, Cheryl Goodman (Assistant Director), Farahnaaz Khakoo-Mausel, Rachel Dunsmoor, Paige Muegenburg, Sushmita Srikanth, Michele Wong, Martin De Alteriis, Cynthia Grant, Jill Lacey, Justin Fisher, David Dornisch, Anna Maria Ortiz, Catherine Hurley, Mark Dowling, Grace Lui, Sarah Veale, Mallory Bulman, David Dayton, David Hancock, Justine Lazaro, and Etana Finkler made key contributions to this report. |

www.ingramcontent.com/pod-product-compliance
Lightning Source LLC
Chambersburg PA
CBHW080540290526
45790CB00006B/2485